PUREST
of All Lilies

The Virgin Mary
in the Spirituality of St. Faustina

Fr. Donald H. Calloway, MIC

PUREST
of All Lilies

The Virgin Mary
in the Spirituality of St. Faustina

By

Fr. Donald H. Calloway, MIC

MARIAN PRESS
STOCKBRIDGE MA 01263
PRO CHRISTO ET ECCLESIA

2008

Available from:
Marian Helpers Center
Stockbridge, MA 01263

Prayerline: 1-800-804-3823
Orderline: 1-800-462-7426
Website: www.marian.org

Imprimi Potest:
Very Rev. Daniel Cambra, MIC
Provincial Superior
Februay 27, 2008

Library of Congress Catalog Number: 2008921624

ISBN: 978-1-59614-195-7

Cover Art: *La Inmaculada Concepción De El Escorial*
Bartolome Esteban Murillo — Catalogue Number 972
· © Museo Nacional del Prado, Madrid
Used with permission

Design of Cover: Br. Angelo Casimiro, MIC
Design of Pages: Kathy Szpak

Editing and Proofreading: Dan Valenti and Mary Flannery

For texts from the English Edition of *Diary of St. Maria Faustina Kowalska*

Nihil Obstat:
George H. Pearce, SM
Former Archbishop of Suva, Fiji

Imprimatur:
Joseph F. Maguire
Bishop of Springfield, MA
April 9, 1984

Printed in the United States of America

*Nothing is too much when it comes
to honoring the Immaculate Virgin.*

St. Maria Faustina Kowalska

This book is dedicated to my dear mother,
LaChita G. Calloway

TABLE OF CONTENTS

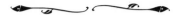

ABBREVIATIONS

AAS	*Acta Apostolicae Sedis. Commentarium officiale.* Rome: Vatican Polyglot Press, 1909-.
Diary	St. Maria Faustina Kowalska, *Diary of Saint Maria Faustina Kowalska: Divine Mercy in My Soul.* (3rd Edition). Stockbridge, MA: Marian Press, 2002.
FADM	Catherine M. Odell, *Faustina: Apostle of Divine Mercy.* Huntington: Our Sunday Visitor, 1998.
Introduction	Jerzy Mrowczynski, *"Introduction"* in *Diary* (2nd edition), 1987.
KDCT	*Konstytucje dotyczace calego Towarzystwa.* Plock, 1909.
LFK	Sr. Sophia Michalenko, C.M.G.T. *The Life of Faustina Kowalska.* Ann Arbor, MI; Servant Publications, 1999.
MFGLM	Vincenzina Krymow, *Mary's Flowers: Gardens, Legends & Meditations.* Cincinnati: St. Anthony Messenger Press, 2002.
OLF	Mabel Maugham (Beldy), *Our Lady's Flowers.* Dublin: Assisi Press, 1958.
SMFK	Maria Tarnawska, *St. Maria Faustina Kowalska: Her Life and Mission.* Stockbridge, MA: Marian Press, 2000.
SSF	Sr. M. Elzbieta Siepak, O.L.M. & Sr. M. Nazaria Dlubak, O.L.M. *The Spirituality of Saint Faustina: The Road to Union with God.* Cracow: Congregation of the Sisters of Our Lady of Mercy, 2000.
TPZ	*Tobie Panie Zaufalem: Modlitewnik Zgromadzenia Siostr Matki Bozej Milosierdzia: Modlitwy w ciagu dnia.* Warszawa, 1986.

INTRODUCTION

During the canonization homily of the first saint of the third Christian millennium, St. Maria Faustina Kowalska (1905-1938), Pope John Paul II noted that this extraordinary woman from Poland was "a gift of God for our times."[1] As a saint whose name is now familiar throughout the Catholic Church, the central charism and mission of St. Faustina was the spread of the Divine Mercy message and devotion. The message and devotion of Divine Mercy, now so well known worldwide, was given to St. Faustina through personal revelations received from Jesus, as recorded in her *Diary*. The core of the message is one of hope for a world greatly in need of forgiveness, compassion, and reconciliation. It is a message, as John Paul II states, "linked for ever to the 20th century, the end of the second millennium and the bridge to the third [millennium]."[2]

Although The Divine Mercy message and devotion are central to understanding the charism and mission of St. Faustina, there are many other facets that constituted her spirituality. Authentic Christian spirituality embraces the whole of Christian life, including the ecclesial, liturgical, sacramental, and apostolic dimensions. One of the most important facets in her overall approach to the spiritual life was her love and devotion to the Blessed Virgin Mary, the Mother of Mercy Incarnate, as Ludmila Grygiel noted: "The characteristics of Sr. Maria Faustina's interior life would be incomplete if we did not mention her Marian devotion."[3] This dimension of her

---

[1] "Sr. Faustina: God's gift to our time," *L'Osservatore Romano* [English Edition] 3 May 2000, p.1

[2] Ibid.

[3] Ludmila Grygiel, *"W Milosierdziu Miary Nie Masz": Rozwazania nad dzienniczkiem siostry Faustyny.* (Kielce, Wydawnictwo Jednosc, 1997), 295. This work has not been translated into English. The English title is translated as: *"In Mercy There Is No Limit": Reflections on the Diary of Sr. Faustina.*

spirituality has often been overlooked due to the primary importance given to her charism and mission in spreading knowledge and devotion to Jesus as The Divine Mercy. Yet, the person of St. Faustina, a woman deeply rooted in the life of the Church, cannot be fully understood without reference to the Marian dimension of her spirituality.

Therefore, this book will examine the Marian dimension of the spirituality of St. Faustina. The Mariological dimensions I will focus on are twofold: the Marian doctrine and Marian devotion in the spirituality of St. Faustina. The overall goal is to show that the Virgin Mary was of major importance, both doctrinally and devotionally, in the spiritual life of St. Faustina.

The primary source of this study consists in the English translation of the critical[4] Polish edition of *Diary of St. Maria Faustina Kowalska: Divine Mercy in My Soul (Dzienniczek: Milosierdzie Boze w Duszy Mojej)* published in 1981.[5] This work is a spiritual masterpiece, and it is quickly becoming a spiritual classic. The secondary sources will be various other studies that have been done on the life of St. Faustina.

---

[4] The critical edition of the *Diary* was only published in 1981. "Critical" means that after having thoroughly analyzed and studied the *Diary*, the various reviewers and editors of the text are offering to the public the authentic version of what St. Faustina wrote. In addition, it contains such things as a critical apparatus, extensive footnotes, and biographical information. In the original preface to the 1981 Polish edition, Andrew Cardinal Deskur, noted the following: "In presenting this edition of the Diary of [Saint] Faustina Kowalska I am fully aware that I am introducing a document of Catholic mysticism of exceptional worth, not only for the Church in Poland, but also for the Universal Church. This publication is the critical edition, and thus reliable. It is the work of the Postulator [Fr. Antoni Mruk, S.J.] of Sister Faustina, under the direction of the authority of the Archdiocese of Cracow." (See *Diary*, xi).

[5] St. Maria Faustina Kowalska, *Diary of Saint Maria Faustina Kowalska: Divine Mercy in My Soul.* (Stockbridge, MA: Marian Press, 2002 [3rd edition]. All citations from the *Diary* will correspond to the paragraph numbers of the *Diary*, not the page numbers.

CHAPTER I

St. Maria Faustina Kowalska

Biographical Sketch

I n every age, God has His way of making something great out of a chaotic beginning. The history of St. Faustina is no different. Born in a land described as "God's playground" and the "heart of Europe"[6] in a time when, yet once again, there was no Poland on the map of Europe, Helen Kowalska (1905-1938) has brought not only glory to God, but honor and prestige to her native land; she is the first native born Polish woman to be canonized in the more than 1,000-year history of Christianity in her native land. Her name is now known throughout the world, and the message of Divine Mercy has quickly swept through the Church.

Early Years

Helen Kowalska was born on August 25, 1905, in a small village in central Poland called Glogowiec. Sr. Sophia Michalenko, a noted biographer of St. Faustina, has aptly noted the paradoxical connotations in the name of the town in which St. Faustina was born. She states: "Glogowiec" comes from the word "glog," a hawthorne berry; or, in a larger sense, weeds or brambles. The hawthorne is a spring shrub or tree of the apple family, noted for its pink and white fragrant flowers. Whether the name describes the village accurately is immaterial; but in God's providence, a "flower" did blossom from the "weeds and brambles" of this humble village.[7]

In order to understand the little girl Helenka (the

---

[6] Cf. N. Davies, *God's Playground: A History of Poland. Vol.1&2.* (Oxford: Clarendon Press, 1981); Ibid., *Heart of Europe: A Short History of Poland.* (Oxford: Oxford University Press, 1984).

[7] Sr. Sophia Michalenko, CMGT, *The Life of Faustina Kowalska: The Authorized Biography.* (Ann Arbor: Servant Publications, 1999), 13. This work was originally printed under the title, *Mercy My Mission: Life of Sister Faustina H. Kowalska, S.M.D.M.* (Stockbridge, MA: Marian Press, 1987).

diminutive of Helen, and what she was often called by family and friends), it is necessary to understand the family situation in which she was raised. Her father, Stanislaus Kowalski, was born on May 6, 1868, in the central Polish village of Swinice, not far from the textile city of Lodz. Trained to be a carpenter by trade, he was a simple yet pious man. St. Faustina's mother, Marianna Babel (Kowalska) was born in a village near Swinice called Mniewie on March 8, 1875. Seven years younger than Stanislaus, she too was simple and pious. Stanislaus and Marianna were married on October 28, 1892, in the bride's hometown of Mniewie. Shortly after their marriage, they made the short trip of two miles to the village of Glogowiec.

The daily life of the Kowalski house consisted of carpentry and farming. Most days Stanislaus was occupied with his carpentry skills to such a degree that Marianna, the loving and hard-working wife, would walk to bring him a hot lunch no matter where he was working. Stanislaus was a hard-working man. Besides his carpentry profession, he also owned about five acres of pasture on which he had a few cows, and about seven acres of farmland on which he grew potatoes and other vegetables. He never missed Sunday Mass or parish feasts, even though it required a lengthy walk to the village church. He was a sincerely devout man who owned numerous books about saints, and he had an enthusiastic regime of daily prayer. Marianna, though illiterate, was the heart of the home. She kept the small brick cottage, consisting of two rooms, a kitchen and two bedrooms, tidy and orderly. Yet, above all, the one thing Stanislaus and Marianna longed for were children.

For the first nine years of their marriage, they remained childless. Things would change, however, when, with the help of the prayers of Madame Babel, Marianna's mother, Stanislaus and Marianna would have 10 children! The first of these children was Josephine (b. 1901). This pregnancy was difficult for Marianna. The second child, also posing difficulties in childbirth, was Genevieve (b. 1903). As a result of these first two difficult deliveries, Marianna was nervous when she became pregnant again with her third child, knowing that if precedent followed, the labor with this child would also be problematic. However, the delivery of this child occurred with no complications, and the child received the name of Helen (b. 1905). So amazed was Marianna at the easy labor during the birth of their third child that she would say years later that the delivery of Helen sanctified her womb. All the seven subsequent pregnancies went well, though some of the children died in infancy: Kazimiera (b. 1907) died in infancy, Natalie (b. 1908), Bronislawa (year of birth unknown), Stanislaus (b. 1912), Mieczyslaw (b. 1915), Marianna (b. 1916), and Wanda (b. 1920). On August 27, 1905, two days after her birth, little Helen was baptized in St. Casimir's Church in Swinice Warckie by Fr. Joseph Chodynski. Her godparents were Maria Szewczyk Szczepaniak and Marcin Lugowski.

POLITICAL MILIEU

The political atmosphere in which Helen was born was one in which most of her native Poland was under Russian occupation. As a matter of fact, the biographer Catherine Odell has noted: "In 1906 there really was no Poland on the map of Europe."[8] Poland has always, from its very beginning, been a land caught between political ideologies. Catherine Odell offers the following as an historical sketch of the political situation into which little Helen was born:

> In 1772, the country [Poland] had lost a third of its territories to its neighbors — Austria, Prussia, and Russia. In 1793, Russia and Prussia had robbed Poland of even more territory. Lithuania and the Ukraine, on Poland's eastern side, were added on to Russia. And on the west, Prussia took most of western Poland. In 1795, the three neighboring nations simply carved up what was left of the Polish middle. As a nation, Poland disappeared.

[8] Catherine M. Odell, *Faustina: Apostle of Divine Mercy.* (Huntington: Our Sunday Visitor, 1998), 18.

The Poles revolted in 1863, five years before the birth of Stanislaus in Swinice. Russia had begun to draft Polish men into its army and the Poles couldn't take this latest insult to their national identity. But Russia cracked down viciously on the rebels. The Russian language was made the official language of the regions near Lodz and to the east of Kowalski's native village. In 1871, Prussia formed the German Empire. Poles under Prussian rule in the west were forced to adopt the German language.

By the twentieth century, men like Stanislaus Kowalski had hidden their political feelings and dreams. And hopes for Poland were kept quietly alive inside the cottages. All official documents — including baby Helen's birth certificate — were written in Russian, in the conqueror's language. And while the Poles prayed for the rebirth of their nation, the people were sustained by a tenacious religious faith. That fed their spirits, just as the coarse rye bread and potatoes sustained their bodies.[9]

The Russian occupation and control of both the economic and political atmosphere certainly was felt by the Kowalski family. Helen, herself, was trained in Polish culture and language. Yet the Russian occupation did have an element to play in Helen's lack of education. In an anecdotal fashion, Fr. Seraphim Michalenko, MIC, has noted:

Until World War I, the section of Poland where Helen lived was under the oppressive rule of the Russians. An indication of the gravity of the oppression was that the Russians prohibited the Polish people from conducting schools in their own language, and so for most Poles in that sector of the country there was no formal education. Once the war was under way, however, Russian rule was dis-

---

[9] *FADM,* 18-19.

mantled, and the people started to school their children in Polish. Starting in 1917, Helen went to school for three terms, beginning in the second grade since she had learned to read at home. However, in order to make room for younger children, she and other older children had to leave school in 1919.[10]

FAMILY MARIAN DEVOTIONS

Undoubtedly, despite her meager education, Helen learned the most important things in life from her parents. From her mother she learned her prayers and her catechism. Her father, for his part, was an avid reader and, though poor, held a small collection of books about such things as the lives of saints and other aspects of Christian life. Stanislaus even made it a practice to gather the family together to read various stories to them, the fruit of which was that young Helen would repeat these heroic stories of saints to her friends. It is well documented that Stanislaus also had a custom of beginning his day with a Marian devotion, as Sr. Sophia Michalenko remarks: "Though he [Stanislaus] did carpentry work during the day, and attended to this farm work afterward (often working well into the night), nevertheless Stanislaus was known to rise very early and begin each day with the singing of the traditional Little Hours of the Immaculate Conception, popularly known as 'Godzinki.'"[11]

This public manifestation of Marian devotion would have a big impact on Helen. For example, when on one occasion during her childhood she awoke early in the morning in order to take the cows out for pasture so that her father did not have to work so hard, she was heard singing the

---

[10] Fr. Seraphim Michalenko, MIC, "The Road to Canonization," in *Pillars of Fire in My Soul: The Spirituality of Saint Faustina*. (ed.) Robert A. Stackpole. (Stockbridge, MA: Marian Press, 2003), 150.

[11] *LFK*, 15; The noted biographer Maria Tarnawska even notes that Stanislaus' practice of singing the "Godzinki" was year round. See *St. Maria Faustina Kowalska: Her Life and Mission*. Trans. Anne Hargest-Gorzelak (Stockbridge, MA: Marian Press, 2000), 23.

"Godzinki" in imitation of her father's daily morning ritual. Interestingly enough, her father thought the cows had been stolen and once he found out Helen had taken them out, he was going to scold her because of the damage the cattle might have done to the crop of rye. However, he was stupefied when he heard his little Helen singing the "Godzinki" and the cows walking right next to the rye crop and only eating the grass.

From the beginning of Helen's life, she was surrounded by Marian devotion. As is well known, Poland has always had wayside shrines to Our Lady, often emphasizing a devotion particular to a given area. Yet, since the Kowalski family was a devout family, even praying the Rosary together, they did not have to go far to express their devotion to Our Lady, as Maria Tarnawska notes:

> In May there were the May devotions to the Blessed Virgin Mary, and again in October, the month of the Rosary. Because it was some way to the church, and May devotions and the Rosary may be said at home, [Stanislaus] Kowalski made a little shrine and fixed it to the pear tree standing on the track outside his home. The children, especially Helenka, would decorate the holy picture with flowers and the whole family and their neighbours would gather there for communal prayers.[12]

Sisters Elzbieta Siepak and Nazaria Dlubak make note of the following in regard to the Marian dimension in the Christian spirituality of the Kowalski family:

> The Kowalski family had the custom of singing the Litany of Loreto together in May and of saying the Rosary in October. In the room in which the family prayed there was a statue of Our Lady next to the crucifix before which the family would kneel every day, and in front of the house on the pear-tree there hung a little shrine around which they would gather

---

[12] *SMFK*, 23.

to pray during the summer months.[13]

The Marian element was, indeed, a powerful influence in the formative years of the Christian journey of Helen. For example, even at the early age of five, Helen often told her mother of dreams she had where she was walking with the Blessed Virgin Mary hand-in-hand in a most beautiful garden.[14] Her family, for their part, often found these dreams hard to believe.

AN EARLY CALLING

At the tender age of seven, Helen experienced a call to religious life, as she would recount years later in her *Diary*: "From the age of seven, I experienced the definite call of God, the grace of a vocation to the religious life. It was in the seventh year of my life that, for the first time, I heard God's voice in my soul; that is, an invitation to a more perfect life. But I was not always obedient to the call of grace. I came across no one who would have explained these things to me."[15]

In 1914, at the age of nine, little Helen received her first Holy Communion at the hands of the local parish priest, Fr. Pawlowski. This first encounter with the Eucharistic Jesus would prove to be the beginning of a wonderful devotion she would have to the Blessed Sacrament. Even as a young girl, she would face in the direction of the church, where she knew the Blessed Sacrament was, as she did her night prayers in the family home.

As a young girl of 10, Helen greatly empathized with the poor. She would often dress up in rags and go door-to-door begging for money and food for the poor. Concerning her education, she was only able to attend two or three sessions of schooling due to her late age in getting started. These years

---

[13] Sr. M. Elzbieta Siepak, OLM & Sr. M. Nazaria Dlubak, OLM, *The Spirituality of Saint Faustina: The Road to Union with God*. Trans. Sr. M. Nazareta Maleta, OLM & Sr. M. Caterina Esselen, OLM (Krakow: Congregation of the Sisters of Our Lady of Mercy, 2002), 85.

[14] See *LFK*, 16; FADM, 19.

[15] *Diary*, 7.

were from 1917 to 1919, between the ages of 12 and 14, respectively.[16] For the next two years, 1919-1921, Helen helped her family in their daily tasks involving in-house work, gardening, and agriculture.

WORKING YEARS

At the age of 15, Helen received permission from her parents to go to the nearby town of Aleksandrow, a town of about 10,000 people, and work for a neighbor's sister, Mrs. Helen Goryszewska. During her time working as a maid, Helen fulfilled her duties well. Interestingly, Mrs. Goryszewska was fond of the way Helen told her son stories about saints and heroes of the faith — this was most likely a skill Helen had learned from listening and watching her father as he did this for the Kowalski household. Helen only stayed in Aleksandrow for about one year.

Upon returning home, Helen requested of her parents permission to enter the convent, but they were vehemently opposed, giving the excuse of lacking money to provide the dowry needed to enter religious life. Actually, however, it was because of their attachment to Helen. After this refusal, Helen left for work again. The year was 1922, and she went to the city of Lodz to live with her cousins, the Rapackis. She worked, though, for some women who belonged to the Third Order of St. Francis. During her time in Lodz, she was able to attend daily Mass and was under the direction of Fr. Wyzykowski, the confessor of the women for whom she worked. Helen's desire for the religious life became stronger and stronger and, after having worked in Lodz for about a year, she again returned home to ask her parents to let her enter religious life.

Upon returning home at the age of 18, Helen posed her question to her parents. Once again, they opposed her request. Years later, in one of the first entries in her *Diary*, St. Faustina would recall her response to her parents refusal to her request: "After this refusal, I turned myself over to the vain things of life, paying no attention to the call of grace, although my soul found

---

[16] See *LFK*, 7, 19.

no satisfaction in any of these things. The incessant call of grace caused me much anguish; I tried, however, to stifle it with amusements. Interiorly, I shunned God, turning with all my heart to creatures."[17] On Feb. 2, 1923, Helen left home again and began working for Mrs. Marcianna Sadowska in Lodz. Mrs. Sadowska had three small children and Helen was to work as a maid and nanny. Once again, Helen exhibited her skill of telling the little children stories, especially religious ones, and won the admiration of all. As a matter of fact, Helen's religious fervor was so apparent that "Mrs. Sadowska could not help but notice that Helen abstained from meat every Wednesday, Friday, and Saturday. During Lent, she ate no meat at all, and also abstained from dairy products on Wednesday, Friday, and Saturday."[18] Helen ceased working for Mrs. Sadowska on July 1, 1924.

SURRENDER TO THE WILL OF GOD

The crucial turning point in the vocational calling of Helen seems to have occurred sometime in the late summer of 1924. She records that one evening while she was attending a dance, most likely held in the city of Lodz, she had a vision of a suffering and sorrowful Jesus in which He addressed her with the words: "How long shall I put up with you and how long will you keep putting Me off?"[19] Upon experiencing this vision of Jesus, Helen immediately left the dance and made her way to the Cathedral of Saint Stanislaus Kostka. Once there, she prostrated herself in front of the tabernacle and begged the Lord to be good enough to give her to understand what she should do next. She then heard these words: "Go at once to Warsaw; you will enter a convent there."[20]

---

[17] *Diary*, 8.

[18] *LFK*, 22. Sr. M. Elizabeth Siepak, in the 'Introduction' to the 3rd English Edition of the *Diary*, notes that St. Faustina practiced "exhausting fasts" before entering religious life. See 'Introduction', xvii.

[19] *Diary*, 9.

[20] Ibid., 10.

It seems Helen did not delay at all about going to Warsaw. As a matter of fact, she did not even say goodbye to her parents. She informed her Uncle and a sister about her immediate need to depart for Warsaw, and her Uncle went with her to the train station. It was a sad departure, and she wept profoundly as the train pulled away. So convinced was she that she had to respond to the call of Jesus that she embarked on the journey with only one dress, the one she was wearing.

Upon arriving in Warsaw by train, Helen became frightful of the big city. She knew no one in Warsaw. After asking the Blessed Virgin Mary for guidance, crying out, "Mary, lead me, guide me,"[21] she received internal guidance to safe lodging for the night outside the city of Warsaw. The next day she returned to the city and entered the first Church she saw — the Church of St. James in Ochota, where an inner voice directed her to speak with the pastor, Fr. James Dabrowski. He sent Helen to a Mrs. Aldona Lipszyc in nearby Ostrowek. Mrs. Lipszyc had four children and, in addition, was taking care of some of her sister's children, and was in need of a maid. Mrs. Lipszyc readily accepted Helen and also provided her with some additional clothing. During the time that Helen was working as a maid, she would go as often as she could into Warsaw and knock on convent doors seeking admittance. However, everywhere she kept meeting with refusal, as she would recount later: "At whatever convent door I knocked, I was turned away."[22]

By Divine Providence, Helen one day knocked on the convent door of the Sisters of Our Lady of Mercy located at 3/9 Zytnia Street in Warsaw. Mother Michael Moraczewska met with Helen and took a liking to the pleasant, freckle-faced strawberry blond with gray-green eyes, but informed her that before she would be accepted she ought to earn funds to provide for a modest wardrobe for the time of probation. Thus Mother Moraczewska recommended that Helen continue to work until she could come up with the needed money. Helen readily agreed to pursue this task, remaining in

[21] Ibid., 11.

[22] Ibid., 13.

the employment of the Lipszyc family.[23]

Helen worked for almost one year saving up the needed money. She continued living a prayerful and ascetic life, even while living in the world. Her heart was truly on fire for a more perfect way of life, and on June 25, 1925, during Vespers of the Octave of Corpus Christi, she made a vow of perpetual chastity. Years later, she wrote in her *Diary* that "from that moment I felt a greater intimacy with God, my spouse. From that moment I set up a little cell in my heart where I always kept company with Jesus."[24] A deepening of the interior life had awakened in Helen.

SISTERS OF OUR LADY OF MERCY

On the vigil of the feast of Our Lady of the Angels, Aug. 1, 1925, Helen entered postulancy with the Congregation of Sisters of Our Lady of Mercy. Helen was extremely grateful for her vocation and put her whole heart and soul into responding to the call of Jesus. The central charism of the Sisters of Our Lady of Mercy was that of caring for wayward girls, and in France, where the community was originally founded, this consisted mainly in helping former prostitutes. Thus they were often called the Magdalenes.

The spirituality of the Congregation was based upon a devotion to the Blessed Virgin Mary as Mother of Mercy, and the apostolate of corporal and spiritual works of mercy. The community also had a strong Eucharistic element, having a tradition of making Eucharistic Holy Hours each Thursday night in reparation for the sins of the world. The patron saints of the community are Our Lady of Mercy, St. Joseph, St. Michael the Archangel, St. Ignatius of Loyola, St. Mary Magdalene, St. Therese of Jesus, and St. Anthony of Padua.

Up until 1962, the Congregation of Sisters of Our Lady of Mercy consisted of two groups, the directresses and the coadjutors. The directresses were those who were well

---

[23] Catherine Odell states that after returning from the meeting with Mother Moraczewska, Helen sang the "Godzinki". See FADM, 40.

[24] *Diary*, 16.

educated and looked to the educational needs of the girls in their charge. The coadjutors were those who did the household chores such as cooking, cleaning, and gardening. Helen, due to her lack of education, was a member of the coadjutors.

INITIAL FORMATION

As a postulant in the house in Warsaw, Helen was assigned to kitchen duty. After only three weeks in postulancy, she wanted to leave the community and join a stricter order, but she came to know for certain that Jesus had called her to this particular religious community. Helen's postulancy ended on April 29, 1926, and she was sent to the Sisters' convent in Lagiewniki near Krakow to begin her novitiate. This convent had been founded in 1890 by Fr. Alexander Lubomirski and served as both the community novitiate and one of the largest houses where the community carried out its charism of helping wayward girls.

Helen entered the novitiate on April 30, 1926. During the ceremony, she was vested in the habit of a novice and received a new name: Sr. Maria Faustina.[25] During her two-year novitiate Sr. Faustina was assigned to kitchen duty. She often found this kind of work difficult and challenging, especially the handling of large pots. During the end of her first year of novitiate, she seems to have entered into a 'dark night' of the soul. On April 30, 1928, she made her first profession of temporary vows, and after remaining in Lagiewniki for six months, received her first assignment of working in the kitchen in the convent in Warsaw, the very same convent where she had been a postulant.

LIFE AS A RELIGIOUS

The move of Sr. Faustina to Warsaw would be the beginning of many moves that she would experience in religious life, some for work-related reasons, others for health reasons. The

---

[25] Sr. Michalenko has noted that the name Faustina means "fortunate, happy or blessed one". See *LFK*, 32. Also, according to endnote #105 of the 3rd English edition of the *Diary*, "there is no custom in the Congregation [Sisters of Our Lady of Mercy] of adding a cognomen to the religious name. But it is possible for a sister to make an addition to her name, depending on the devotion she has, as, for instance, Sister Faustina did, when she added "of the Blessed Sacrament."

many places she lived were Warsaw, Krakow, Vilnius, Kiekrz, Plock, Walendow, and Derdy. In most of the places that she lived, she served either in the kitchen, in the garden, or as the portress. In the life of Sr. Faustina there were two priests in particular who served as her spiritual directors and confessors. They were Fr. Joseph Andrasz, SJ,[26] (assigned to be the quarterly confessor to the Sisters in Lagiewniki in 1932), and Fr. Michael Sopocko,[27] whom she met in Vilnius. These saintly priests would prove to play an essential part in the mission and spiritual journey of Sr. Faustina.

Her final vows of poverty, chastity, and obedience were made on May 1, 1933, in the presence of Bishop Stanislaus Rospond. Sadly, she had no family or guests at this great moment in her life. As a matter of fact, after having seen her parents one last time in 1935, she never saw them again. Both of her parents outlived her, and it was due to her long-time suffering from tuberculosis of the lungs and the alimentary system that she died in the convent in Krakow on October 5, 1938. She was only 33 years old. Her funeral was held on October 7, 1938 (the feast of Our Lady of the Rosary) and no one from her family attended. As history would have it, "she was hardly mentioned for two years following her death."[28]

---

[26] Fr. Joseph Andrasz, SJ was born in Zakopane, Poland on October 16, 1891. He entered the Society of Jesus on September 22, 1906 and was ordained to the priesthood on March 19, 1919. In his early years as a priest he worked in a publishing house and eventually became the editor of the monthly magazine "Messenger of the Sacred Heart" (*Poslaniec Serca Jezusowego*). From 1932, he was the extraordinary confessor of the novices of the Sisters of Our Lady of Mercy in Lagiewniki near Krakow. He heard Faustina's last confession on October 5, 1938. He died on February 1, 1963.

[27] Fr. Michael Sopocko was born on November 1, 1888 in Nowosady, a town near Vilnius. He studied at the Catholic Seminary in Vilnius and was ordained to the priesthood on June 14, 1914. He did higher studies at both the School of Theology of the Warsaw University and at the Pedagogical Institute; during World War II he served as a seminary professor in Bialystok. He was the ordinary confessor to the Sisters of Our Lady of Mercy in Vilnius from January 1, 1933 to January 1, 1942. He died on February 15, 1976 in Bialystok. His cause for canonization began in 1987, and the Holy See recognized his heroic virtues in 2004.

[28] *LFK.,* 273.

AFTER DEATH

When Poland was invaded on September 1, 1939, it was almost impossible for people to find out about Sr. Faustina and the message of Divine Mercy. Fr. Julian Chrosciechowski, MIC, gives a concise historical sketch of the times:

> The political situation throughout occupied Poland made it very difficult to spread the devotion to Divine Mercy. It was, indeed, quite impossible to publicize the Message of Mercy in Western Poland, which had been annexed to the Reich, and in which Polish churches were closed, and their priests murdered, imprisoned or deported. In these circumstances, it was impossible to do much to spread the devotion. Conditions were better in Central Poland, which was ruled by the Germans as a separate administrative unit known as the General Government. Here the Poles were allowed a certain amount of religious freedom, and many of them came to hear of the devotion, although all Catholic periodicals — indeed, all Polish publications — were banned. The devotion spread, however, quite spontaneously.[29]

After World War II ended, Fr. Joseph Andrasz, SJ, and Fr. Michael Sopocko both wrote books on the life of St. Faustina and The Divine Mercy message and devotion. Both of these books brought the person and mission of St. Faustina to a post-war world. However, on March 6, 1959, the Congregation of the Holy Office (now called the Sacred Congregation for the Doctrine of the Faith) issued a notification banning the writings about Divine Mercy (the *Diary*) as given to Sr. Faustina.[30] This ban, lasting some 20 years, was

---

[29] Fr. Julian Chrosciechowski, MIC, *Devotion to Divine Mercy in our Day: A Historical and Critical Study.* Second Edition. Trans. R. Batchelor. (Stockbridge, MA: Marian Press, 1976), 88-89. Cf. Fr. Julian Chrosciechowski, MIC, "The Devotion to the Divine Mercy," *American Ecclesiastical Review* 132 (April, 1955): 264-275.

[30] AAS, 51 (1959), 271.

revoked on April 15, 1978.[31] The primary reason for the ban had been erroneous translations.

Beatification and Canonization

Even during the years of the ban, however, an Informative Process into the life of Sr. Faustina was opened under the leadership of Archbishop Karol Wojtyla on October 21, 1965, in the Krakow Diocese. At this stage Sr. Faustina was considered a 'Servant of God.' As a result of the Informative Process, the mortal remains of Sr. Faustina were exhumed from their resting place in the convent cemetery on November 25, 1966, and interred inside the convent chapel in Lagiewniki. The Informative Process took two years and was closed on September 20, 1967. On January 31, 1968, the Beatification Process began. Also during this time, Fr. Ignacy Rozycki, an eminent theologian and later a member of the International Theological Commission, was requested by the Archbishop of Krakow to study the *Diary* of Sr. Faustina. His research took ten years.[32]

Three years after the ban on her writings was lifted, a woman from the United States, Mrs. Maureen Digan, claimed to have been healed of terminal lymphedema through the intercession of Sr. Faustina.[33] Years would go by before Maureen's healing would be declared a miracle on Dec. 21, 1992.[34] Earlier in that year, March 7, 1992, the heroic virtues of Sr. Faustina were recognized and she was declared a Venerable Servant of God.[35] Things proceeded fairly quickly after that and the Venerable Servant of God was beatified by Pope John Paul II in St. Peter's Square on April

---

[31] AAS, 70 (1978), 350.

[32] Sacra Congregatio Pro Causis Sanctorum, *Faustinae Kowalska*, (Cracovien, 1979).

[33] Congregatio de Causis Sanctorum, (P.N. 1123), "De Instantanea et perfecta sanatione Dominae Maureen Cahill Digan a morbo v.d. "Chronic Lymphedema". Die 28 Martii 1981", (Roma: 1991). Cf. Maureen Digan, "Story of a Miracle," *The Association of Marian Helpers Bulletin*, (Winter, 1992-3): 5-7.

[34] *AAS*, 85 (1993), 390-392.

[35] *AAS*, 84 (1992), 926-929; See, also, "Sr. Faustina now Venerable," *The Association of Marian Helpers Bulletin*, (June/July, 1992): 12-13.

18, 1993 (Divine Mercy Sunday).[36]

On Oct. 5, 1995 (the feast day of the then-Blessed Faustina), a priest from the Archdiocese of Baltimore, Maryland, Fr. Ronald Pytel, was instantaneously healed of an enlarged left ventricle of the heart. He attributed the healing to the intercession of Bl. Faustina, with whose relic he was blessed at the end of a day of prayer for his healing. After much investigation into the alleged healing, the Holy See affirmed its miraculous nature on Dec. 20, 1999.[37] Thus, on April 30, 2000 (Divine Mercy Sunday), Bl. Faustina was canonized the first saint of the new millennium.[38] Pope John Paul II also declared during the celebration that the Second Sunday of Easter would now be known as Divine Mercy Sunday. Saint Maria Faustina was solemnly declared by her community to be a co-foundress who "re-founded or, in other words, founded anew her maternal Congregation."[39]

---

[36] *L'Osservatore Romano* [English Edition], 21 April 1993: 1-3.

[37] *AAS*, 92 (2000), 422-424. Cf. Congregatio de Causis Sanctorum, (P.N. 1123), "Positio Super Miraculo" (Roma, 1999).

[38] *AAS*, 92 (2000), 670-674.

[39] *SSF*, 71.

CHAPTER II

The Virgin Mary in the Spirituality
of St. Maria Faustina

The role of the Virgin Mary in the spirituality of St. Faustina is one of vital importance. In her desire to be conformed to Christ, her living out of the Christian life, especially through the evangelical counsels, followed a distinctively Marian character. This Marian dimension in the spirituality of St. Faustina is easily evidenced when one reads through the pages of her *Diary* and, as Maria Tarnawska rightly notes, "It would be an incomplete picture of the spiritual life of Sister Faustina that did not include the role that Our Lady played in it."[40]

Mariologists have commonly referred to the age in which St. Faustina grew up as the "Age of Mary."[41] Polish culture in itself has a long history of instilling a love for the Virgin Mary in the hearts of its faithful.[42] Other significant Marian happenings during the lifetime of St. Faustina include the Fatima apparitions (1917), the Legion of Mary founded by Frank Duff in Ireland (1921), the Beauraing apparitions (1932/33), the Feast of the Divine Motherhood was established (1931), and the Banneux apparitions (1933).

A comprehensive study on the overall position of the Virgin Mary in the spirituality of St. Faustina has not been done. In fact, such a severe lack of investigation into the Marian dimension of the spirituality of St. Faustina exists that the primary reason Fr. George Kosicki, CSB, undertook the project of compiling a thematic index to the *Diary* was to show the abundant quantity of Marian references that exists in the *Diary*.[43]

Another source for determining the Marian dimension in the spirituality of St. Faustina was the community that she

---

[40] *SMFK,* 341.

[41] Cf. René Laurentin, *The Question of Mary.* Trans. I.G. Pidoux (New York: Holt, Rinehart and Winston, 1965), pp.9-52. Originally published as *La Question Mariale* (Editions du Seuil, 1963).

[42] It should be remembered that in 1656 King John Casimir proclaimed Mary as Queen of Poland, and in 1966, the one-thousandth year anniversary of the coming of Christianity to Poland, the entire nation elected Mary as Queen of Poland.

[43] Cf. George W. Kosicki, CSB, *Study Guide to the Diary of St. Maria Faustina Kowalska.* (Stockbridge, MA: Marian Press, 1996), 6.

joined, the Congregation of Sisters of Our Lady of Mercy. The *Constitutions* of the Congregation of Sisters of Our Lady of Mercy are a rich source for coming to understand the Marian dimension in the life of this community and will be referred to frequently in this chapter and in the next. However, suffice it to note here that in the 1930 *Constitutions* (Chapter 1, paragraph 7 "On the Goal and Spirit of the Congregation") the following is put forth as a major component in the spirituality of the Congregation:

> This very spirit [the apostolic aims of the Congregation] the Sisters will nourish by frequent meditation on the works of salvation for the human race, as well as the virtues and sentiments of the Merciful God's Mother — whose patience, sweetness and motherly pity towards sinners the Sisters will strive to imitate.[44]

Accordingly, this chapter will seek to present the overall Marian dimension in the spirituality of St. Faustina.

EUCHARISTIC-MARIAN SPIRITUALITY

St. Faustina understood the simple, yet profound, truth that without the Virgin Mary there would be no Incarnation and, thus, no Eucharistic presence of Jesus. For example, in two poetic passages she states the notion that the flesh of both the Incarnation and the Eucharistic presence of Jesus come through Mary:

> Unfathomable and incomprehensible in Your mercy,
> For love of us You take on flesh

---

[44] *Konstytucje Sióstr Zgromadzenia NMP Milosierdzia* [Constitutions of the Sisters of Our Lady of Mercy] (Warszawa, 1930), 6.

From the Immaculate Virgin, ever untouched by sin,
Because You have willed it so from all ages.[45]

And

O Sacred Host, fountain of divine sweetness,
You give strength to my soul;
O You are the Omnipotent One, who took flesh
    of the Virgin,
You come to my heart, in secret,
Beyond reach of the groping senses.[46]

St. Faustina was fully aware that to love Jesus in the Eucharist one must have a sincere love for that person through whom Jesus comes to us, the Virgin Mary. Two beautiful poetic passages reveal that St. Faustina understood Mary to be the first tabernacle of the Body and Blood of Jesus:

Your beauty [Mary] has delighted the eye
    of the Thrice-Holy One.
He descended from heaven, leaving His
    eternal throne,
And took Body and Blood of Your heart
And for nine months lay hidden in a Virgin's Heart.

O Mother, Virgin, purest of all lilies,
Your heart was Jesus' first tabernacle on earth.[47]

And

You [God] have indeed prepared a tabernacle for
Yourself: the Blessed Virgin. Her Immaculate Womb
is Your dwelling place, and the inconceivable miracle
of Your mercy takes place, O Lord. The Word
becomes flesh; God dwells among us, the Word of
God, Mercy Incarnate.[48]

---

[45] *Diary*, 1746.
[46] Ibid., 1233.
[47] Ibid., 161.
[48] Ibid., 1745.

These are profound reflections upon the relationship of Mary and the Eucharist. With such an understanding of the interconnection of Mary in the mystery of Christ's Incarnation-Eucharistic presence, it is no wonder that St. Faustina stated: "before every Holy Communion I earnestly ask the Mother of God to help me prepare my soul for the coming of Her Son."[49]

St. Faustina's experiences with the Eucharist necessarily add a liturgical dimension to her spirituality. It should not be surprising to find, therefore, a liturgical dimension in her love for the Virgin Mary. Through even a brief perusal through her *Diary* it becomes readily apparent that many, perhaps most, of the encounters that St. Faustina had with Our Lady occurred during a liturgical celebration, whether it was a liturgical feast of Our Lord[50] or of Our Lady. In the spirituality of St. Faustina, there is no separating Jesus from His Mother. They always go together.

Fr. Adam Sikorski, MIC, has noted that Faustina's encounters with Mary within the liturgical year take on the form of a "sacramental" due to their disposing Faustina to an ever deeper union with God through sacramental grace.[51] By following the liturgical year, we note that St. Faustina's favorite time of the year was undeniably Advent. Maria Tarnawska, commenting on the fervor with which St. Faustina prepared herself for the reception of Holy Communion, remarked: "An especially intensive period of prayer for Faustina was Advent, the liturgical period serving to make ready the soul for the birth of the Infant Jesus. Sister Faustina took this duty [the reception of Jesus in Communion and at Christmas] very seriously so that even more than usual she would ask the Holy Mother of God to help her and direct her in accomplishing this duty."[52]

---

[49] Ibid., 1114.

[50] E.g., she depicts Our Lady as present on the Lord's feast of the Ascension. See *Diary*, 1710-1711.

[51] See Adam Sikorski, MIC, "Maria nella Vita Spirituale e nel Messaggio della Serva di Dio Suor Maria Faustina Kowalska (1905-1938)," in *De Culto Mariano Saeculis XIX-XX: Acta Congressus Mariologici-Mariani Internationalis in SanctuarioMariano Kevelaer (Germania) Anno 1987 Celebrati: Vol. VI. Roma:* Pontificia Academia Mariana Internationalis, 221.

[52] *SMFK,* 348.

Mary herself seems to have instructed St. Faustina in a more intense way during Advent. Thus, it is not surprising that St. Faustina will frequently note things like:

- "The Mother of God has taught me how to prepare for the Feast of Christmas,"[53]

- "I will spend this Advent in accordance with the directions of the Mother of God,"[54]

- "I am awaiting Christmas with great yearning; I am living in expectation together with the Most Holy Mother,"[55]

- "I am spending this time with the Mother of God and preparing myself for the solemn moment of the coming of the Lord Jesus,"[56]

- "Advent is approaching. I want to prepare my heart for the coming of the Lord Jesus ... uniting myself with the Most Holy Mother."[57]

St. Faustina mentions her great love for Christmas so often that it can be considered a hallmark of her liturgical spirituality.

The other liturgical celebration that always occurs in Advent is the Solemnity of the Immaculate Conception; Maria Tarnawska called it St. Faustina's "favorite Feast of Our Lady."[58] St. Faustina would prepare for this liturgical celebration as much as two months in advance.[59] In her zeal for preparing for this feast she would, and did on three occasions, make a novena of 9,000 *Hail Mary's*![60]

---

[53] *Diary*, 785. Cf. SSF, 98.
[54] Ibid., 792.
[55] Ibid., 829.
[56] Ibid., 840.
[57] Ibid., 1398.
[58] *SMFK*, 346.
[59] See *Diary*, 805.
[60] See *Diary*, 1413.

Outside of the liturgical season of Advent, some of the other celebrations that St. Faustina frequently mentions in reference to her encounters with Mary are Feb. 2 (Purification of Mary/Presentation of Jesus),[61] March 25 (Annunciation),[62] Aug. 5 (Our Lady of Mercy),[63] and Aug. 15 (Assumption).[64] She will also mention her "May devotions"[65] and the times she visited Czestochowa.[66] In essence, in her desire to become like Jesus in the Eucharist, St. Faustina knew that she had to go through Mary and incorporate her into all the key components of her spirituality.

CO-SUFFERING

In her desire to become sacrificial like the Eucharist, St. Faustina often reflected upon the sorrows that Mary experienced during her lifetime. For example, during Vespers on Nov. 30, 1936, when St. Faustina was undergoing a piercing pain in her soul, the Mother of God appeared to her and stated:

> Know, My daughter, that although I was raised to the dignity of Mother of God, seven swords of pain pierced My heart. Don't do anything to defend yourself; bear everything with humility; God Himself will defend you.[67]

The Virgin Mary was a constant source of strength for St. Faustina as she underwent various trials, sufferings, and purifications on her spiritual journey. On Feb. 2, 1937, the

---

[61] See *Diary*, 913-916, 1558.

[62] See *Diary*, 635

[63] See *Diary*, 266, 449.

[64] See *Diary*, 325, 468, 677, 1206, 1244.

[65] See *Diary*, 1704.

[66] See *Diary*, 260, 521.

[67] *Diary*, 786. There are many variations of the seven sorrows of Mary, but in 1482, Fr. John de Coudenberghe, a parish priest in Flanders, standardized the following seven sorrows by his preaching: 1) The Prophecy of Simeon (Lk.2:34-35), 2) The Flight into Egypt (Mt.2:13-21), 3) The Loss of Jesus for Three Days (Lk.2:41-50), 4) The Ascent to Calvary (Jn.19:17), 5) The Crucifixion and Death of Jesus (Jn.19:18-30), 6) Jesus Taken Down from the Cross (Jn.19:39-40), 7) Jesus Laid in the Tomb (Jn.19:40-42). See *Dictionary of Mary*. (New Jersey: Catholic Book Publishing Co., 1997), 445-446.

Feast of the Purification of Mary,[68] St. Faustina relates how she looked to Mary as a source of strength in sufferings, because Mary herself underwent excruciating suffering during her earthly journey:

> O Mary, today a terrible sword has pierced Your Holy soul. Except for God, no one knows of Your suffering. Your soul does not break; it is brave, because it is with Jesus. Sweet Mother, unite my soul to Jesus, because it is only then that I will be able to endure all trials and tribulations, and only in union with Jesus will my little sacrifices be pleasing to God. Sweetest Mother, continue to teach me about the interior life. May the sword of suffering never break me. O pure Virgin, pour courage into my heart and guard it.[69]

As we will explore later in this chapter, many of the insights concerning suffering came to Faustina through Mary at a particular liturgical celebration. For instance, repeating the theme of the sword of sorrow, Faustina related on the First Friday of September 1937, that Mary appeared to her with "breast bared and pierced with a sword."[70] She will also relate how on Christmas Eve, 1937, she was able to experience the anxiety of the Virgin as she prepared to give birth to her divine Son.[71]

The spiritual suffering Mary went through during her earthly journey is something real and concrete for St. Faustina, and she knew that Mary underwent all of this suffering out of love for Jesus and souls. Mary even instructed St. Faustina to unite herself closely with the Holy Sacrifice of the Mass as an offering,[72] and to "fix your gaze upon the Passion of My Son."[73]

---

[68] At the time, February 2 was celebrated and titled 'The Purification of Mary'. However, after the liturgical changes of Vatican II, the title of this feast was changed to 'The Presentation of the Lord'.

[69] *Diary*, 915.

[70] Ibid., 686.

[71] See *Diary*, 1437.

[72] See *Diary*, 325.

[73] *Diary*, 449. Cf. *Diary*, 561.

On occasion, Mary even prepared St. Faustina for sufferings that were to come. For example, in 1934 she noted the following:

> Mother of God, Your soul was plunged into a sea of bitterness; look upon Your child and teach her to suffer and to love while suffering. Fortify my soul that pain will not break it. Mother of grace, teach me to live by [the power of] God.

> Once, the Mother of God came to visit me. She was sad. Her eyes were cast down. She made it clear that She wanted to say something, and yet, on the other hand, it was as if She did not want to speak to me about it. When I understood this, I began to beg the Mother of God to tell me and to look at me. Just then Mary looked at me with a warm smile and said, *You are going to experience certain sufferings because of an illness and the doctors; you will also suffer much because of the [Divine Mercy] image, but do not be afraid of anything.* The next day I fell ill and suffered a great deal, just as the Mother of God had told me. But my soul was ready for the sufferings. Suffering is a constant companion of my life.[74]

Mary did not leave St. Faustina alone in her sufferings, however. For her part, Mary often expressed in tender language the fact that she, as mother, was with St. Faustina in her suffering. For example, Mary often expressed her maternal affection for St. Faustina in her suffering moments by using such phrases as: "I feel constant compassion for you,"[75] "I sympathize with you,"[76] and "I know how much you suffer, but do not be afraid. I share with you your suffering, and I shall always do so."[77] All of this was meant to express Mary's maternal solicitude for St. Faustina as a co-suffering mother, and St. Faustina was always aware of Mary's

---

[74] Ibid., 315-316.

[75] *Diary*, 805.

[76] Ibid., 635.

[77] Ibid., 25.

presence: "She alone is always with me. She, like a good
Mother, watches over all my trials and efforts."[78]

Faustina, for her part, was instructed by Mary to practice
the co-suffering virtue of compassion.[79] As Dr. Robert
Stackpole, S.T.D., has stated: "Co-redemptive suffering became
the very heart of her vocation."[80]

IMMACULATE VIRGIN

The role of Mary in St. Faustina's desire to become pure,
like the white Eucharistic-host, is undeniably the most promi-
nent role of Mary in the entire *Diary*. Concerning this, Maria
Tarnawska has rightly noted, "Above all the requests she
brought to Our Lady one was foremost: that the Immaculate
Mother would protect her from the temptations of the flesh."[81]
It can be said that St. Faustina's greatest desire was to be pure.
She referred to Mary as "Immaculate" a total of 17 times in her
Diary,[82] and even described her own love as 'immaculate'
(*niepokalana*).[83] Jesus himself requested the following from her,
stating: "My daughter, I want to delight in the love of your
heart, a pure love, virginal, unblemished, untarnished."[84]

Certainly St. Faustina learned to look to Our Lady as a
means to attaining purity because the *Constitutions* of the
Congregation of Sisters of Our Lady of Mercy often stress this
point. For example, in both the *Constitutions* of 1909 and
1930 we read the following:

> With respect to the vow of chastity, suffice it to say,
> they who choose Jesus Christ as Spouse, the
> Immaculate Mother of God as Lady and model,

[78] Ibid., 798.

[79] Ibid., 1244.

[80] Robert Stackpole, *Jesus, Mercy Incarnate: St. Faustina and Devotion to Jesus
Christ.* (Stockbridge, MA: Marian Press, 2000), 65.

[81] *SMFK*, 344.

[82] See *Diary*, 161, 564, 805-806, 843, 874, 1097, 1232, 1410-1414, 1745,
1746.

[83] See *Diary*, 159.

[84] *Diary*, 279.

and St. Joseph as a special patron, they ought to imitate as far as possible the purity of the very angels, preserving purity of body and soul.[85]

The way of life expressed through the *Constitutions* was not something abstract for Faustina.[86] For example, we note that she understood Mary's importance in helping one attain chastity when she stated that one must have a "sincere devotion to the Blessed Virgin Mary."[87]

The preeminent privilege that St. Faustina sought to contemplate and imitate in Mary is her purity, her immaculateness. St. Faustina referred to the Immaculate Conception of Our Lady 12 times in her *Diary*. The Immaculate Conception was for St. Faustina a model and mirror upon which she desired to pattern herself. For this reason, she recorded that in the years 1935, 1936, and 1937, she greatly prepared for and celebrated the Solemnity of the Immaculate Conception. These passages offer great insights into St. Faustina's strong desire for a purity comparable to that of the Immaculate One. Here I will cite these passages in chronological order:

> (1935) On the feast of the Immaculate Conception of the Mother of God, during Holy Mass, I heard the rustling of garments and saw the most holy Mother of God in a most beautiful white radiance. Her white garment was girdled with a blue sash. She said to me, *You give me great joy when you adore the Holy Trinity for the graces and privileges which*

---

[85] *Konstytucje dotyczace calego Towarzystwa* [Constitutions pertaining to the entire Association]. (Plock, 1909), 50; *Konstytucje Sióstr Zgromadzenia NMP Milosierdzia* [Constitutions of the Sisters of Our Lady of Mercy] (Warszawa, 1930), 36.

[86] Interestingly, one particular charism of the Congregation of Sisters of Our Lady of Mercy was the daily obligation to pray the 'Little Hours of the Immaculate Conception'. This was the prayer that her father prayed every morning when she lived at home. Regarding this daily obligation, the 1909 *Constitutions* note: "All the Sisters will daily pray the Little Hours of the Immaculate Conception. They will pray them with respect, reflection and devotion, as such a holy work demands." See KDCT, 66.

[87] *Diary*, 93.

were accorded Me. And She immediately disappeared.[88]

(1936) From early morning, I felt the nearness of the Blessed Mother. During Holy Mass, I saw Her, so lovely and so beautiful that I have no words to express even a small part of this beauty. She was all [in] white, with a blue sash around Her waist. Her cloak was also blue, and there was a crown on Her head. Marvelous light streamed forth from Her whole figure. *I am Queen of heaven and earth, but especially the Mother of your [Congregation].* She pressed me to Her heart and said, *I feel constant compassion for you.* I felt the force of Her Immaculate Heart which was communicated to my soul. Now I understand why I have been preparing for this feast for two months and have been looking forward to it with such yearning. From today onwards, I am going to strive for the greatest purity of soul, that the rays of God's grace may be reflected in all their brilliance. I long to be a crystal in order to find favor in His eyes.[89]

(1937) It is with great zeal that I have prepared for the celebration of the Feast of the Immaculate Conception of the Mother of God. I have made an extra effort to keep recollected in spirit and have meditated on that unique privilege of Our Lady. And thus my heart was completely drowned in Her, thanking God for having accorded this great privilege to Mary. I prepared not only by means of the novena said in common by

---

[88] Ibid., 564.
[89] Ibid., 805.

the whole community,[90] but I also made a personal effort to salute Her a thousand times each day, saying a thousand "Hail Marys" for nine days in Her praise. This is now the third time I have said such a novena to the Mother of God: that is, a novena made up of a thousand Aves each day. Thus the novena consists in nine thousand salutations. Although I have done this now three times in my life, and two of these while in the course of my duties, I have never failed in carrying out my tasks with greatest exactitude. I have always said the novena outside the time of my exercises; that is to say, I have not said the *Aves* during Holy Mass or Benediction. Once, I made the novena while lying ill in the hospital. Where there's a will, there's a way. Apart from recreation, I have only prayed and worked. I have not said a single unnecessary word during these days. Although I must admit that such a matter requires a good deal of attention and effort, nothing is too much when it comes to honoring the Immaculate Virgin.

The Feast of the Immaculate Conception. Before Holy Communion I saw the Blessed Mother inconceivably beautiful. Smiling at me She said to me, *My daughter, at God's command I am to be, in a special and exclusive way your Mother; but I desire that you, too,*

---

[90] St. Faustina's Congregation prayed the novena *'Nowenna przed Uroczystoscia Niepokalanego Poczecia Najswietszej Maryi Panny'* [Novena before the Feast of the Immaculate Conception of the Most Blessed Virgin Mary] beginning on November 29. See *Tobie Panie Zaufalem: Modlitewnik Zgromadzenia Sióstr Matki Bozej Milosierdzia: Modlitwy w ciagu dnia* [In You, O Lord, I Place My Trust: Prayer Book of the Sisters of the Merciful Mother of God: Prayers during the day] (Warszawa, 1986), 83-85. See Appendix for the text of the novena to the Immaculate Conception.

*in a special way, be My child. I desire, My dearly
beloved daughter, that you practice the three
virtues that are dearest to Me — and most
pleasing to God. The first is humility, humility,
humility, and once again humility; the second
virtue, purity; the third virtue, love of God. As
My daughter, you must especially radiate with
these virtues.* When the conversation ended,
She pressed me to Her heart and disappeared.
When I regained the use of my senses, my
heart became so wonderfully attracted to
these virtues; and I practice them faithfully.
They are as though engraved in my heart.[91]

The above excerpts offer many examples of how Mary, in
her entire person, personified purity for St. Faustina, for
example, the white dress,[92] Mary's beauty,[93] the light sur-
rounding Mary,[94] the Immaculate Heart, and the metaphor of
the 'crystal.'

Other instances of St. Faustina's understanding that
Mary's Immaculate Conception served as her model of purity[95]
are seen in her poetic praise of Mary. Although St. Faustina's
poetic style of expressing doctrinal and devotional truths will be
analyzed in chapters three and four, certain passages where this
applies to her understanding of Mary's Immaculate Conception
should be quoted here. The following quotes, presented in
chronological order, strongly accent Mary's purity:

(1934) O Mary, Immaculate Virgin,
     Pure crystal for my heart,
     You are my strength, O sturdy anchor!

---

[91] *Diary*, 1412-1415. In entry 1624 [March 1, 1938], St. Faustina noted: "This
month I will practice the three virtues recommended to me by the Mother of God:
humility, purity and love of God."

[92] Mary often appeared to St. Faustina wearing a white dress. Cf. *Diary*, 564, 677,
805-806, 1585

[93] St. Faustina often asserted that Mary's beauty is incomparable. Cf. *Diary*, 161,
325, 449, 805, 1414.

[94] Cf. *Diary*, 805-806, 1232, 1442.

[95] *Diary*, 874.

You are the weak heart's shield and
protection.

O Mary, You are pure, of purity
incomparable;
At once both Virgin and Mother,
You are beautiful as the sun, without
blemish,
And Your soul is beyond all comparison.

Your beauty has delighted the eye of the
Thrice-Holy One.
He descended from heaven, leaving His
eternal throne,
And took Body and Blood of Your heart
And for nine months lay hidden in a
Virgin's Heart.
O Mother, Virgin, purest of all lilies,
Your heart was Jesus' first tabernacle on
earth.[96]

(1937) O sweet Mother of God,
I model my life on You;
You are for me the bright dawn;
In You I lose myself, enraptured.

O Mother, Immaculate Virgin,
In You the divine ray is reflected,
Midst storms, 'tis You who teach me to
love the Lord,
O my shield and defense from the foe.[97]

(1938) Unfathomable and incomprehensible in
Your mercy,
For love of us You take on flesh

---

[96] Ibid., 161.

[97] Ibid., 1232. In some ways, this poetic prayer is similar to the *Respice stellam* of
St. Bernard of Clairvaux (1090-1153). See In *Laudibus Virginis Matri Hom. in
Opera Omnia Vol.IV.,* 35.

From the Immaculate Virgin, ever
untouched by sin,
Because You have willed it so from all ages.[98]

All throughout her religious life, St. Faustina sought to obtain purity through the intercession of Mary. From two specific passages in her *Diary* it does, indeed, appear that Mary did obtain this gift for her special daughter. For example, in a retrospective account, St. Faustina noted that in 1929 the Lord Jesus gave her a "belt of purity" and affectionately noted the following:

Since then [after receiving the belt of purity] I have never experienced any attacks against this virtue [chastity], either in my heart or in my mind. I later understood that this was one of the greatest graces which the Most Holy Virgin Mary had obtained for me, as for many years I had been asking this grace of Her. Since that time I have experienced an increasing devotion to the Mother of God.[99]

The last thing that needs to be mentioned concerning the greatness with which St. Faustina held purity, especially as exemplified in the Virgin Mary, is the fact that when she encountered St. Joseph in visions she saw him as an "Old Man."[100] Depicting St. Joseph as an old man has often been a way of safeguarding the virginity and purity of Mary. It is interesting that at Midnight Mass in 1937, Faustina related explicitly that St. Joseph did not even see the birth of Christ:

When I arrived at Midnight Mass, from the very beginning I steeped myself in deep recollection, during which time I saw the stable of Bethlehem filled with great radiance. The Blessed Virgin, all

---

[98] Ibid., 1746.

[99] Ibid., 40. Years later in entry 1097 (April, 1937) she will note: "Since that time [the reception of the belt of purity], I have been living under the virginal cloak of the Mother of God. She has been guarding me and instructing me. I am quite at peace, close to Her Immaculate Heart."

[100] See *Diary*, 608, 846.

lost in the deepest of love, was wrapping Jesus in swaddling clothes, but St. Joseph was still asleep. Only after the Mother of God put Jesus in the manger, did the light of God awaken Joseph, who also prayed.[101]

From this passage, we are left to understand that no creature was able to see the intact and perpetual purity of the Virgin in childbirth. Mary's purity is truly a mystery that makes the angels cry out: "Glory to His Mother, the humble and pure Virgin."[102]

HUMILITY, HUMILITY, HUMILITY

St. Faustina learned humility both from Jesus, the omnipotent God who became humble bread in the Eucharist, and from the Virgin Mary, the one who, though having an infinite dignity due to her privilege of the Divine Maternity, had the most profound humility. For this reason, in her desire to reciprocate the humility she experienced in the Most Blessed Sacrament, St. Faustina often petitioned the Virgin Mary with the request of a deeper humility: "O Virgin most pure, but also most humble, help me to attain deep humility."[103]

Mary would, on many occasions, instruct St. Faustina about the importance of humility in the spiritual life. For example, one time on the feast of the Ascension (May 26, 1938), Mary told St. Faustina: "The soul's true greatness is in loving God and in humbling oneself in His presence, completely forgetting oneself and believing oneself to be nothing; because the Lord is great, but He is well-pleased only with the humble; He always opposes the proud."[104] This spiritual lesson is strikingly similar to the words uttered by Mary in her Magnificat (Lk. 1:48-55), a Marian passage from Sacred Scripture that St. Faustina knew well from the liturgy.

---

[101] *Diary,* 1442.

[102] Ibid., 1742.

[103] Ibid., 1306.

[104] Ibid., 1711.

The Virgin Mary also counseled St. Faustina on how to acquire humility and meekness through preparing for the Infant Jesus, the humble God, at Christmas,[105] and by bearing "everything with humility."[106] As a matter of fact, the Virgin Mary conveyed in a powerful way that the three virtues most dear to her heart were humility, purity, and love of God:

> I desire, My dearly beloved daughter, that you practice the three virtues that are dearest to Me — and most pleasing to God. The first is humility, humility, and once again humility; the second virtue, purity; the third virtue, love of God. As My daughter, you must especially radiate with these virtues.[107]

St. Faustina understood Mary herself to be a great example of humility and meekness. At certain times, St. Faustina recorded that "the humility and love of the Immaculate Virgin penetrated my soul,"[108] and "my spirit brightens up in Your gentleness and Your humility, O Mary."[109] St. Faustina even portrayed the angels as crying out in praise of the Virgin's humility[110] because, as St. Faustina noted concerning the humility of the Virgin, "Only because no humility was deeper than Yours [Mary] were You raised above the choirs of Angels and above all Saints."[111]

LESSONS ON SILENCE

In her desire to be silent like the Eucharist, St. Faustina understood the Virgin Mary to be a great model. Saint Faustina learned many lessons on the need for silence in the life of a religious from the lips of the Virgin Mary. On one occasion, the Virgin Mary told Faustina that "Your [her Congregation's] lives

---

[105] See *Diary*, 785, 792.

[106] *Diary*, 786. Cf. *Diary*, 1244, 1624.

[107] *Diary*, 1415.

[108] Ibid., 843.

[109] Ibid., 620.

[110] See *Diary*, 1742.

[111] *Diary*, 161.

must be like Mine: quiet and hidden."[112] Also, during Advent of 1936, Mary told St. Faustina to strive after silence and humility in preparation for Christmas.[113]

The lessons on silence given to St. Faustina from the Virgin Mary had a noticeable impact on her spiritual life, as she would seek to live out her Eucharistic-liturgical spirituality in a spirit of silent anticipation. For example, one year (1937), in preparation for Christmas, she noted: "I want to prepare my heart for the coming of the Lord Jesus by silence and recollection of spirit, uniting myself with the Most Holy Mother and faithfully imitating Her virtue of silence, by which She found pleasure in the eyes of God Himself. I trust that, by Her side, I will persevere in this resolution."[114]

In addition, included in the liturgical dimension of her Eucharistic spirituality, St. Faustina mentioned that in 1937, "the flower which I lay at the feet of the Mother of God for May is my practice of silence."[115] Her love for Mary knew no bounds. She even recorded that in preparation for the feast of the Immaculate Conception, she "made an extra effort to keep recollected in spirit,"[116] by not saying a "single unnecessary word."[117] Interestingly, the only thing Mary told her never to be silent about was Divine Mercy: "Speak to souls about this great mercy while it is still time for mercy. If you keep silent now, you will be answering for a great number of souls on that terrible day. Fear nothing."[118]

---

[112] *Diary*, 625.
[113] See *Diary*, 785.
[114] *Diary*, 1398.
[115] Ibid., 1105.
[116] Ibid., 1412.
[117] Ibid., 1413.
[118] Ibid., 635.

TO THE DIVINE MERCY
THROUGH MARY

That St. Faustina understood the Virgin Mary to have a special relationship to The Divine Mercy is given in the very name of her religious community: The Sisters of Our Lady of Mercy. Interestingly, of all the places that The Divine Mercy image could have been displayed for the first time, it was St. Faustina who asked Fr. Sopocko that the image be first displayed at the Ostra Brama[119] chapel in Vilnius, Lithuania.[120]

Furthermore, in her desire to spread the message and devotion to The Divine Mercy, St. Faustina understood that being united with the Virgin Mary was a beneficial way of exalting and making the mercy of God known: "To give worthy praise to the Lord's mercy, we unite ourselves with Your Immaculate Mother, for then our hymn will be more pleasing to You, because she is chosen from among men and angels."[121] St. Faustina offers a profound reason for why Mary is associated with The Divine Mercy, based on the notion of mercy present in Mary's Magnificat (see Lk. 1: 50, 54). Simply put, Mary, due to her Immaculate Conception and her giving birth to Mercy Incarnate, "is first to praise the omnipotence of Your mercy."[122]

On the Feast of Our Lady of Mercy in 1935, Mary revealed to St. Faustina the link between her spiritual motherhood and The Divine Mercy: "I am Mother to you all, thanks to the unfathomable mercy of God."[123] St. Faustina,

---

[119] Ostra Brama or "Dawn Gate" is an image of the Virgin Mary that dates from the early sixteenth century that was hung over the entrance to the gate of the southeastern side of the city of Vilnius. See Joan Carroll Cruz, *Miraculous Images of Our Lady.* (Rockford, Ill: Tan Books, 1993), 266-269.

[120] See *Diary,* 89.

[121] *Diary,* 1746.

[122] Ibid. Cf. John Paul II, *Dives in Misericordia,* 9-10.

[123] Ibid., 449.

indeed, understood Mary to be the "Mother of Mercy"[124] and, thus, greatly associated in both the message and devotion to Jesus, The Divine Mercy.

MODEL OF INTERIOR LIFE

Trust is a virtue that gives one the ability to live a deeply interior life, not being swayed by the many external happenings in life but, rather, seeing all things as the unveiling of Divine Mercy. This is what trust meant for St. Faustina, and within this understanding of trust she looked to Mary as both a model and a teacher in how to live an interior life of trust. The 1909 *Constitutions* of her community even noted that the Sisters are to live out their vocation by "heartfelt reflection on the virtues and sentiments of their Mother and Patroness, the merciful Mother of God."[125]

St. Faustina understood the Virgin Mary, at the supreme moment of human history, that is, the Incarnation, to be a lesson in trusting God's merciful plan of salvation: "She [Mary] believes the words of God's messenger and is confirmed in trust."[126] In this Mary serves as a model and teacher of the interior life, and of that wondrous virtue called trust. As a matter of fact, St. Faustina often referred to Mary as a model: "You are the model and star of my life,"[127] and "I model my life on You."[128]

Interestingly, the Mother of God herself conveyed to St. Faustina in 1936 that she would gain for St. Faustina a deep interior life: "My daughter, I shall obtain for you the grace of an interior life which will be such that, without ever leaving that interior life, you will be able to carry out all your external duties with even greater care."[129] The fact that Mary helped St. Faustina to grow in trust through a deep interior life is a

---

[124] See *Diary*, 330.
[125] *KDCT*, 6.
[126] *Diary*, 1746.
[127] *Diary*, 874.
[128] Ibid., 1232.
[129] Ibid., 785.

constant theme in her *Diary*.[130] This modeling of her life on the Virgin Mary's trust also involved the element of trusting in the midst of sorrow, as is seen when on the Feast of the Presentation in 1937, St. Faustina related how she wanted to be like Mary in her suffering the sword of sorrow, crying out: "Sweetest Mother, continue to teach me about the interior life. May the sword of suffering never break me."[131]

MARY AND THE CHRIST CHILD

In her desire to surrender and become childlike in response to the mercy of God, St. Faustina often portrayed herself as a child of Mary. At times Mary will call St. Faustina her daughter and child,[132] and St. Faustina often referred to herself in filial terms when presenting her relationship with Mary.[133] Aware of her own struggles in the spiritual life, St. Faustina commented in endearing terms, "Because I am so weak and inexperienced, I nestle like a little child close to Her [Mary's] heart."[134]

The filial relationship, which Faustina had with Mary, also included a Christocentric dimension. This is easily seen when one notes that on many of the occasions when St. Faustina saw the Virgin Mary, Mary held the Christ Child in her arms.[135] On one occasion, when St. Faustina seems to have been participating in a novena to Our Lady, she recounts how Mary requested of her a childlike spirit:

> On the evening of the last day [November 15] of the novena at Ostra Brama, after the singing of the litany, one of the priests exposed the Blessed Sacrament in the monstrance. When he placed it on the altar, I immediately saw the Infant Jesus, stretching out His little arms, first of all toward His

---

[130] See *Diary,* 40, 454, 840, 1711.

[131] *Diary,* 915.

[132] See *Diary,* 325, 785-786, 1414.

[133] See *Diary,* 240, 260, 315, 568.

[134] *Diary,* 1097.

[135] See *Diary,* 25, 182, 230, 330, 529, 561, 597, 608, 677, 846, 1585.

Mother, who at that time had taken on a living appearance. When the Mother of God was speaking to me, Jesus stretched out His tiny hands toward the congregation. The Blessed Mother was telling me to accept all that God asked of me like a little child, without questioning; otherwise it would not be pleasing to God. At that moment, the Infant Jesus vanished, and the Mother of God was again lifeless, and Her picture was the same as it had been before.[136]

This childlike trust in the will of God, seeking to carry out all that Jesus asked of her, was made concrete through her relationship with her confessor and spiritual director. Since Faustina understood, in a profound way, that Jesus spoke to her about His will in and through her confessor and spiritual director, it only seems appropriate that at a Mass celebrated by Fr. Andrasz for the Feast of the Assumption (August 15, 1936), we note the following instruction of Mary to St. Faustina: "See with what assurance I entrust Jesus into his [Fr. Andrasz's] hands. In the same way, you are to entrust your soul and be like a child to him [Fr. Andrasz]."[137]

Two liturgical feasts that St. Faustina took special delight in, due to their dealing with the Child Jesus, were the Purification of Mary (Presentation of Jesus) and Christmas. In the year 1936, St. Faustina noted that on both the Feast of the Purification of Mary (February 2) and the Feast of Christmas (December 25), the Virgin Mary presented the divine infant to Faustina, describing Him as her "dearest" and "most precious treasure."[138] On several occasions Mary conveyed to St. Faustina that her "greatest treasure" was the Infant Jesus. All of these instances served to teach St. Faustina that childlike simplicity, received through the maternal mediation of Mary, was to be an essential part of her spiritual life.

---

[136] *Diary,* 529.

[137] Ibid., 677.

[138] Ibid., 608, 846.

MOTHER OF MERCY

According to the *Constitutions* of the Sisters of Our Lady of Mercy, Mary served as the "perfect model" of the apostolic life.[139] Two ways that St. Faustina expressed her understanding of the Mother of Mercy's intercession were for the souls in purgatory and for Poland.

During her postulancy (1925-1926), St. Faustina relates that on one occasion she was given the experience of visiting the souls in purgatory, and while there she witnessed the intercession of Mary:

> I saw my Guardian Angel, who ordered me to follow him. In a moment I was in a misty place full of fire in which there was a great crowd of suffering souls. They were praying fervently, but to no avail, for themselves; only we can come to their aid. The flames which were burning them did not touch me at all. My Guardian Angel did not leave me for an instant. I asked these souls what their greatest suffering was. They answered me in one voice that their greatest torment was longing for God. I saw Our Lady visiting the souls in Purgatory. The souls call her "Star of the Sea." She brings them refreshment. I wanted to talk with them some more, but my Guardian Angel beckoned me to leave. … Since that time, I am in closer communion with the suffering souls.[140]

St. Faustina understood Mary as "Star of the Sea,"[141] bringing the souls in purgatory refreshment, meaning that Mary intercedes for them so that their purification might be quickened. Having experienced this visit to purgatory at the

---

[139] See *KDCT,* 46.

[140] *Diary,* 20.

[141] Mary's title of "Star of the Sea" *(Stella maris)* is an ancient title and was used by such notable persons as St. Jerome (d. 420), Isidore of Seville (d. 636), Alcuin (d. 804), Paschasius Radbertus (d. 865), Hincmar of Reims (d. 882), and St. Bernard of Clairvaux (d. 1153), among others.

beginning of her religious life was undoubtedly a source for her constant intercession for the souls in purgatory. The Marian element also played an important part in her prayers for the souls in purgatory due to the fact she made note that she prayed the Rosary in order to aid the suffering souls.[142] Furthermore, on the Feast of the Assumption in 1937, Mary told St. Faustina that those who persevere faithfully in the community will be spared the fire of purgatory.[143]

The other aspect of how St. Faustina understood Mary to be an interceding Mother of Mercy was in her experiences of both seeing Mary pray for Poland, and being asked by Mary to pray for Poland.[144] A powerful image that undoubtedly left an impression on St. Faustina and impelled her to pray for Poland occurred in September 1936:

> In the evening, I saw the Mother of God, with Her breast bared and pierced with a sword. She was shedding bitter tears and shielding us against God's terrible punishment. God wants to inflict terrible punishment on us, but He cannot because the Mother of God is shielding us. Horrible fear seized my soul. I kept praying incessantly for Poland, for my dear Poland, which is so lacking in gratitude for the Mother of God.[145]

The image of Mary with "breast bared" evokes maternal compassion for her children, and maternal intercession before her divine Son.[146] One must remember that Poland was on the

---

[142] See *Diary*, 314.

[143] See *Diary*, 1244.

[144] Interestingly, St. Faustina noted on two occasions how she fervently prayed for the conversion of Russia. Could this be a reference to a knowledge of Mary's request at Fatima? See *Diary*, 818 and 861. Another interesting fact is that Pope John Paul II, during his time of recuperation in the hospital after having been shot, had two things read to him – the documents of Fatima and the *Diary* of St. Faustina. See *FADM*, 167.

[145] *Diary*, 686.

[146] In the history of Christian art, which is a way of visualizing theology, there has often been the depiction of Christ "showing the wounds" *(ostentatio vulnerum)* to his Father for the benefit of mankind, as a plea for mercy. In addition, there is also the artistic tradition that depicts the Virgin Mary as "showing the breasts"

brink of war at this time, and the atrocities that would occur in Poland in World War II would cause any mother to shed copious tears of intercession.

This was not the only time, however, that St. Faustina saw Mary interceding for Poland.[147] On one occasion when St. Faustina was praying a novena for Poland,[148] she experienced another vision of Mary:

> On the seventh day of the novena I saw between heaven and earth, the Mother of God, clothed in a bright robe. She was praying with Her hands folded on Her bosom, Her eyes fixed on Heaven. From Her Heart issued forth fiery rays, some of which were turned toward Heaven while the others were covering our country.[149]

The Mother of Mercy often requested of St. Faustina that she intercede for Poland.[150] St. Faustina for her part took this injunction of the Mother of God seriously, even pleading to the Heart of Jesus through the intercession of Mary and the saints for her beloved Poland:

> Once, after an adoration for our country, a pain pierced my soul, and I began to pray in this way:

(*ostentatio mammarum*) to her divine Son for the benefit of mankind, as a plea for mercy. Most of these artistic depictions began around the 10th century. See Catharina Film, *"Intercessio Christi" i svensk senmedeltida konst ["Intercessio Christi" in Swedish medieval art]* (Uppsala, 1971). This theological depiction is also evidenced in written form, as in, for example, the following selection from Arnold of Bonneval (d. 1156): "Now man can approach God with confidence, since in the Son he has a mediator of his case with the Father, and with the Son he has [a mediatrix] in the Mother. Christ, his side laid bare, shows the Father his side and his wounds; Mary shows Christ her womb and her breasts; and there is no way man's case can be rejected where these monuments of clemency and tokens of charity are found together, making a request more eloquently than any tongue." See Arnold of Bonneval as quoted in Luigi Gambero, S.M. *Mary in the Middle Ages: The Blessed Virgin Mary in the Thought of Medieval Latin Theologians.* Trans. Thomas Buffer. (San Francisco: Ignatius Press, 2005), 152.

[147] See *Diary*, 1585.

[148] In addition to this novena, St. Faustina also noted that she made a novena before the Feast of the Assumption for the intention of Poland. See *Diary*, 1206.

[149] *Diary*, 33.

[150] See *Diary*, 325 and 468.

"Most merciful Jesus, I beseech You through the intercession of Your Saints, and especially the intercession of Your dearest Mother who nurtured You from childhood, bless my native land. I beg You, Jesus, look not on our sins, but on the tears of little children, on the hunger and cold they suffer. Jesus, for the sake of these innocent ones, grant me the grace that I am asking of You for my country."[151]

THE WILL OF GOD
THROUGH MARY

The desire of St. Faustina to do the will of God in all things had a distinctively Marian character. For St. Faustina, Mary served as a model of surrender to the will of God, teaching her "how to carry out His holy will in all things."[152] In particular, this understanding of Mary as a model of abandonment to the will of God during her life was described by St. Faustina in the liturgical feasts of Christmas (1937) and the Ascension (May 26, 1938):

> [*Christmas Eve*]. After Holy Communion, the Mother of God gave me to experience the anxious concern she had in Her heart because of the Son of God. But this anxiety was permeated with such a fragrance of abandonment to the will of God that I should call it rather a delight than an anxiety. I understood how my soul ought to accept the will of God in all things.[153]

---

[151] *Diary,* 286.
[152] Ibid., 40.
[153] Ibid., 1437.

Today [the Feast of the Ascension] I accompanied the
Lord Jesus as He ascended into heaven. It was about
noon. I was overcome by a great longing for God. It
is a strange thing, the more I felt God's presence, the
more ardently I desired Him. Then I saw myself in
the midst of a huge crowd of disciples and apostles,
together with the Mother of God. ... I saw the
longing of Our Lady. Her soul yearned for Jesus with
the whole force of Her love. But She was so peaceful
and so united to the will of God that there was not a
stir in Her heart but for what God wanted.[154]

In addition to the liturgical feasts in which St. Faustina
came to understand the Virgin Mary as a model of surrender
to the will of God, St. Faustina was also instructed personally
by Mary concerning doing the will of God. This happened
during the two Marian celebrations of Our Lady of Mercy
(Aug. 5, 1935) and the Assumption (Aug. 15, 1937):

I prepared for this feast [Our Lady of Mercy] with
greater zeal than in previous years . . . Then I saw the
Blessed Virgin, unspeakably beautiful. She came
down from the altar to my kneeler and said to me, *I
am Mother to you all, thanks to the unfathomable
mercy of God. Most pleasing to Me is that soul which
faithfully carries out the will of God.* She gave me to
understand that I had faithfully fulfilled the will of
God and had thus found favor in His eyes.[155]

During meditation, God's presence pervaded me
keenly, and I was aware of the Virgin Mary's joy at
the moment of Her Assumption. ... I remained
alone with the Most Holy Mother who instructed
me about the will of God and how to apply it to my
life, submitting completely to His most holy decrees.
It is impossible for one to please God without

---

[154] Ibid., 1710.
[155] Ibid., 449.

obeying His holy will. *My daughter, I strongly recommend that you faithfully fulfill all God's wishes, for that is most pleasing in His holy eyes. I very much desire that you distinguish yourself in this faithfulness in accomplishing God's will. Put the will of God before all sacrifices and holocausts.* While the heavenly Mother was talking to me, a deep understanding of this will of God was entering my soul.[156]

As can be seen from these passages, St. Faustina both modeled her obedience to the will of God on the pattern of Mary's obedience and, at the same time, received personal instructions from Mary concerning doing the will of God.[157] This Marian dimension of seeking to do the will of God is further attested to when we note the other times she petitioned Mary to help her do the will of God.

MARY AND THE PRIESTHOOD

The reliance of St. Faustina on her spiritual director and confessors, always being priests, was of great importance for her as she sought to do the will of God. Notably, the two most important priests in her life were Fr. Michael Sopocko and Fr. Joseph Andrasz, SJ. In a certain sense, her *Diary* not only contains a veritable 'theology of spiritual direction' but also many directives for priests, especially concerning The Divine Mercy message and devotion. Yet, there was also a strong Marian dimension when it comes to St. Faustina's relations with the priests in her life.

St. Faustina presents Mary as having a great love for priests. For example, on the feast of the Assumption in 1936, St. Faustina remarked that in a vision during the Mass of Fr. Andrasz, she beheld Mary handing the infant Jesus to Fr. Andrasz and then "looking at Father [Andrasz] with great tenderness."[158] In addition, on the feast of the Immaculate

---

[156] Ibid., 1244. Cf. *Diary*, 635.

[157] See *Diary*, 170, 1624.

[158] *Diary*, 677.

Conception of that same year, she noted: "I saw a certain priest [most likely Fr. Sopocko or Fr. Andrasz] who was surrounded by the light which flowed from Her [Mary]; evidently, this soul loves the Immaculate One."[159]

St. Faustina made it a point to mention the special relationship existing between Fr. Andrasz and the Virgin Mary.[160] St. Faustina heard from his lips the following instructions when she went to him for spiritual direction: "Place yourself in the hands of the Most Holy Mother."[161] Fr. Andrasz was considered to be a holy priest by St. Faustina, and in a revealing passage she tells us why he was holy:

> During one time of prayer, I learned how pleasing to God was the soul of Father Andrasz. He is a true child of God. It is rare that divine sonship shines forth so clearly in a soul, and this because he has a special devotion to the Mother of God.[162]

St. Faustina also recounted the close relationship that Fr. Sopocko had with the Mother of God. For example, on one occasion St. Faustina had a vision in which she saw Fr. Sopocko celebrating Mass and the divine Infant and Mary were there. During this vision Mary "shielded him [Fr. Sopocko] with Her cloak and said, *Courage, My son, courage.*"[163] St. Faustina often prayed for both Fr. Sopocko and Fr. Andrasz, and even prayed

---

[159] Ibid., 806.

[160] Interestingly, Fr. Andrasz, commenting on the vision that St. Faustina had on March 25, 1936 (*Diary,* 635) where Mary tells St. Faustina that she is to prepare the world for the second coming of Christ, makes the following remarkable statement regarding the eschatological nature of this vision: "It [the eschatological vision on March 25, 1936] exhibits much of the great importance of Our Lady's apparitions at La Salette, Lourdes, and lately in Fatima, and, it would seem, even surpasses them in this respect." See Joseph Andrasz, SJ, *Divine Mercy . . . We Trust in You!* trans. Fr. Seraphim Michalenko, MIC (Stockbridge, MA: Marian Press, 1986), 40.

[161] *Diary,* 1243. In *Diary* entry 637 St. Faustina is told by an unnamed confessor: "You are going through life with the Mother of God, who faithfully responded to every divine inspiration."

[162] Ibid., 1388.

[163] Ibid., 597. The theme of Mary covering souls with her cloak/mantle is very prominent in the *Diary* of St. Faustina and will be fully analyzed in the next chapter.

a novena to Our Lady of the Assumption for the intentions of
Fr. Sopocko.[164]

Though she doesn't provide the specific names of the priests
in the following episodes, we can assume that they were either Fr.
Sopocko or Fr. Andrasz. These accounts note the great love that
Mary has for priests. The first account was written in 1934:

> Once, the confessor told me to pray for his inten-
> tion, and I began a novena to the Mother of God.
> This novena consisted in the prayer, "Hail, Holy
> Queen," recited nine times. Toward the end of the
> novena I saw the Mother of God with the Infant
> Jesus in Her arms, and I also saw my confessor
> kneeling at Her feet and talking with Her. I did not
> understand what he was saying to Her, because I was
> busy talking with the Infant Jesus, who came down
> from His Mother's arms and approached me. I could
> not stop wondering at His beauty. I heard a few of
> the words that the Mother of God spoke to him [the
> confessor] but not everything. The words were: *I
> am not only the Queen of Heaven, but also the Mother
> of Mercy and your Mother.* And at that moment She
> stretched out her right hand, in which She was
> clasping her mantle, and She covered the priest with
> it. At that moment, the vision vanished.[165]

The themes presented in this vision are revelatory of
Mary's love for priests. Priests are her sons, and she speaks with
them in tender maternal words, encouraging them and remind-
ing them that although she is Queen she is also Mother of
Mercy and the Mother of priests. This later theme is prominent
in the second passage, in which St. Faustina recorded a mysterious vision concerning Our Lady and her priest sons:

> [A vision of the Mother of God.] In the midst of a
> great brilliance, I saw the Mother of God clothed in

---

[164] See *Diary,* 1206.
[165] *Diary,* 330.

a white gown, girt about with a golden cincture; and there were tiny stars, also of gold, over the whole garment, and chevron-shaped sleeves lined with gold. Her cloak was sky-blue, lightly thrown over the shoulders. A transparent veil was delicately drawn over her head, while her flowing hair was set off beautifully by a golden crown which terminated in little crosses. On Her left arm She held the Child Jesus. A Blessed Mother of this type I had not yet seen. Then She looked at me kindly and said: *I am the Mother of God of priests.* At that, She lowered Jesus from Her arm to the ground, raised Her right hand heavenward and said: *O God, bless Poland, bless priests.* Then She addressed me once again: *Tell the priests what you have seen.* I resolved that at the first opportunity of seeing Father I would tell; but I myself can make nothing of this vision.[166]

This is undeniably one of the most mysterious visions in the entire *Diary.* In a certain sense, this image of Mary can be considered the Marian image that is to be the counterpart to the image of The Divine Mercy, in which Jesus is dressed in a seamless priestly robe; Jesus is the priest, Mary is the Mother of priests. Mary is, indeed, the Mother of priests, and she wants them to know this truth. Priests stand in a special relationship to Mary because they have a share in her divine Son's priesthood. To date, little has been done to promote this image of Our Lady as given to St. Faustina.

LESSONS ON OBEDIENCE

For St. Faustina doing the will of God meant obeying all legitimate authority, especially the Church, her religious superiors, and her spiritual directors and confessors. By surrendering her will and being obedient she became fruitful in the spiritual life and allowed herself to be an instrument in the saving plan

---

[166] Ibid., 1585. The phrase "Mother of God of priests" is somewhat odd, but this is an exact translation from the Polish: *Jestem Matka Boska Kaplanska.*

of Christ. Concerning obedience in the life of a religious, Jacques Servais has insightfully noted: "Obedience in the consecrated life does not have only the ascetic or functional significance that one normally ascribes to it; rather, it possesses a properly co-redemptive virtue."[167] St. Faustina fully lived out the co-redemptive dimension of obedience.

Since St. Faustina understood that "it is impossible for one to please God without obeying His holy will,"[168] she patterned her surrender to God on Our Lady's *fiat*, the apex of Christian obedience. For example, in her *Diary* we find four passages that are similar in wording to Mary's *fiat* obedience:

> Do with me as You please. I subject myself to Your will. As of today, Your holy will shall be my nourishment, and I will be faithful to Your commands with the help of Your grace. Do with me as You please.[169]

> Deign to hear the sighs of Your dearly beloved. Oh, how I suffer because I am still unable to be united with You. But let it be done according to Your wishes.[170]

> Jesus, I ask You, give me the strength for battle. Let it be done to me according to Your most holy will. My soul is enamored of Your most holy will.[171]

> O sweet, rose-red blood of Jesus, ennoble my blood and change it into Your own blood, and let this be done to me according to Your good pleasure.[172]

These four excerpts reveal that St. Faustina had a Marian *fiat* structure to her obedience. Just as Mary was obedient to the angel and said, "Be it done unto me according to your word" (Lk. 1:38), so St. Faustina offered this same response

---

[167] Jacques Servais, "The Evangelical Counsels and the Total Gift of Self," *Communio: International Catholic Review* 31 (Fall, 2004), 372.

[168] *Diary,* 1244.

[169] Ibid., 136.

[170] Ibid., 867.

[171] Ibid., 1498.

[172] Ibid., 1575.

to God, which allowed her to cooperate in His redemptive plan through obedience to His will.

Maria Tarnwaska's words concerning Mary's overall role in the life of St. Faustina seem most appropriate:

> It would indeed be difficult to over-estimate the role of the Most Holy Mother in the life of Sister Faustina. As she felt it, Jesus was inextricably linked with His Mother. In order to fulfill His will, therefore, one should stay as close to her as possible. This is what in fact she did.[173]

---

[173] *SMFK*, 353.

CHAPTER III

Marian Doctrine in St. Faustina's Spirituality

It is helpful to approach the Mariological content found in the *Diary* from a doctrinal understanding. Though St. Faustina was certainly not an academic theologian, nevertheless, her frequent writings and reflections about the Virgin Mary portray many dimensions of the role of the person of the Virgin Mary in the life of the Church. In other words, contained within the strong Marian dimension of the Christocentric spirituality of St. Faustina are many doctrinal themes related to Marian studies.

Perhaps the best way to approach this subject is to present the material as found in the *Diary* in a thematic schema. St. Faustina touches upon most of the Marian doctrines, some to a greater extent than others. In light of this, this chapter will analyze how St. Faustina's Marian spirituality underscores certain Marian doctrines that hold an important place in the life of any Christian.

DIVINE MOTHERHOOD

One of the strongest Marian doctrines St. Faustina constantly affirms in her *Diary* is that Mary is the Mother of God. This great title of Our Lady is used by St. Faustina no less than 66 times.[174] This title and role of Mary can truly be considered the preeminent way that St. Faustina understood both the dignity of Mary and her role in relation to Jesus. No other creature has this privilege.

---

[174] See *Diary,* 11, 25, 33, 40, 170, 182, 240, 260, 315, 316, 325, 330, 346, 468, 529, 561, 564, 597, 608, 635, 637, 677, 686, 728, 785, 792, 795, 798, 840, 843, 846, 1097, 1105, 1114, 1232, 1244, 1250, 1388, 1412, 1413, 1437, 1442, 1558, 1585, 1624, 1710. The paragraphs cited refer to Faustina's explicit use of "Mother of God." It should be noted, however, that she refers to Mary's maternal role in relation to Jesus, using various ways of describing it, a total of 78 times.

In keeping with her liturgical spirituality, St. Faustina often presented Mary's Divine Motherhood within the liturgical feasts that depict this, for example, the Annunciation, Christmas, and the Presentation in the Temple. Thus, in order to present her understanding of various elements of the Divine Motherhood, each of these feasts as they appear in the *Diary* will now be examined.

Firstly, in one of her poetic moments, St. Faustina offered an exalted understanding of the Divine Motherhood at the Annunciation:

> He [Jesus] descended from heaven, leaving His
>   eternal throne,
> And took Body and Blood of Your heart
> And for nine months lay hidden in a Virgin's Heart.
>
> Oh Mother, Virgin, purest of all lilies,
> Your heart was Jesus' first tabernacle on earth.[175]

This statement reveals that the instrument of our salvation, the Body and Blood of the God-man, truly "took flesh of the Virgin."[176] Hers was a real maternity due to the fact that for nine months the Word of God was hidden within her. Interestingly, St. Faustina uses the symbol of the heart when employing the word 'tabernacle.'[177]

St. Faustina also understood that the privilege of being the Mother of God came both from God's desire and Mary's surrender in faith. Mary herself told St. Faustina on the feast of the Annunciation in 1936 that she "gave the Savior to the world."[178] At the same time, since Mary is not a mere passive instrument in the Incarnation of the Word, St. Faustina rightly noted that Mary, at the Annunciation, "believes the words of God's messenger and is confirmed in trust."[179]

---

[175] *Diary*, 161.

[176] Ibid., 1233.

[177] She will also describe Mary's womb as a tabernacle. See *Diary*, 1745.

[178] *Diary*, 635.

[179] Ibid., 1746.

While in no way earning or claiming a right to the Divine Motherhood, nonetheless, St. Faustina understood that Mary was called to actively cooperate in the bringing about of the Incarnation, and this through her belief in God's revelation. Thus, St. Faustina completely understood that Jesus is truly both the Son of God and the Son of Mary.

Concerning the feast of Christmas, in which Mercy Incarnate became visible to the world, St. Faustina often reflected deeply on the mystery of Mary's Divine Motherhood. Christmas was, without a doubt, the feast in which St. Faustina often elaborated upon Mary's Divine Motherhood.[180]

Perhaps one of the most interesting facets of how St. Faustina presented Mary's Divine Motherhood was that it also entailed great spiritual suffering, because of her intimate association with the mission of her divine Son. For example, during Advent of 1936, the Mother of God told St. Faustina the following: "Know, My daughter, that although I was raised to the dignity of Mother of God, seven swords of pain pierced My heart."[181] Being the Mother of God is a wonderful privilege, but it also brought with it a heavy responsibility and a co-suffering mission with the Messiah. For this reason, the association of the role of the Divine Motherhood with suffering was apparent to St. Faustina: "Mother of God, Your soul was plunged into a sea of bitterness; look upon Your child and teach her to suffer and to love while suffering."[182] In short, what St. Faustina deeply understood about Mary's Divine Motherhood was that it carried with it the added privilege of suffering with and for Christ.

In a similar way, St. Faustina also understood Mary's Divine Motherhood as seen at the feast of the Purification of Mary (Presentation in the Temple) to be another revelation of the suffering associated with the Divine Motherhood. For example, on this feast in 1937, she noted:

O Mary, today a terrible sword has pierced Your

---

[180] See *Diary,* 182, 346, 785, 829, 840, 843-846, 1398, 1437.

[181] *Diary,* 786.

[182] Ibid., 315.

holy soul. Except for God, no one knows of Your
suffering.[183]

This passage reveals that Faustina understood the
prophecy of Simeon (cf. Lk. 2:33-35) to refer to the suffering
that Mary would undergo because of her role as the Mother
of God. In this sense, Mary's role as Mother of God is not one
in which only her body was involved. On the contrary, due to
the fact that she shared intimately in the redemption of
mankind as Mother of God, St. Faustina also understood that
Mary's Divine Motherhood involved not just her physical
union with Christ but also an intimate moral union through
her will and intellect.

SPIRITUAL MATERNITY

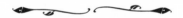

A consequence of the Divine Motherhood is Mary's role as
spiritual mother of God's people. St. Faustina deeply understood that, because of Mary's intimate maternal union with
the Savior, there also existed an intimate maternal union
between Mary and Christian disciples. For example, within
the *Diary* we note that she refers to Mary as "spiritual" mother
20 times,[184] to herself as the daughter of Mary 11 times[185] and
the terminology of "child" 5 times.[186]

On one occasion Mary told St. Faustina that her role as
spiritual mother is part of the will of God: "My daughter, at
God's command I am to be, in a special and exclusive way your
Mother; but I desire that you, too, in a special way, be My

---

[183] Ibid., 915.

[184] See *Diary*, 25, 79, 161, 220, 240, 260, 330, 798, 844, 915, 1114, 1414.

[185] See *Diary*, 325, 568, 785-786, 846, 1244, 1414-1415.

[186] See *Diary*, 240, 260, 315, 1097, 1414.

child."[187] Knowing that Mary's role as personal spiritual mother in regard to St. Faustina was the will of God gave St. Faustina the understanding that she could entrust all of her cares and concerns to Mary, her spiritual mother. Maternity was part of the capacity God had given to the Virgin Mary, namely, to be a maternal presence in the spiritual life, one that nourished, protected, and taught St. Faustina how to grow closer to God.

The maternal presence of Mary in the life of St. Faustina was concrete. For example, on Dec. 9, 1936, she noted: "She [Mary], like a good Mother, watches over all my trials and efforts."[188] In addition, the theme of Mary acting as a mother who guards, protects, and instructs her children in the spiritual life is a prominent one in the *Diary*.[189] St. Faustina even referred to Mary as "Instructress"[190] and "Mother of grace."[191]

Another interesting facet of how St. Faustina understood Mary's spiritual motherhood is that, much like her Divine Motherhood in which she co-suffered with Christ, she shares in the sufferings of her children. This theme comes up at least three times in the *Diary*,[192] giving clear evidence that St. Faustina understood Mary's role as spiritual mother to be that of bringing comfort to her. Perhaps the clearest example of this dimension of Mary's spiritual motherhood can be seen in the following passage: "I know how much you suffer, but do not be afraid. I share with you your suffering, and I shall always do so."[193]

---

[187] *Diary*, 1414. Cf. *Diary*, 240.

[188] Ibid., 798.

[189] See *Diary*, 79, 161, 240, 315, 798.

[190] See *Diary*, 620.

[191] See *Diary*, 315. Cf. *Lumen Gentium*, 61.

[192] See *Diary*, 25, 316, 805.

[193] *Diary*, 25.

MEDIATION/INTERCESSION

Mary's role as spiritual mother is also seen in the life of St. Faustina through the aspects of maternal mediation and intercession. Just as St. Faustina herself was called by Jesus to be a messenger of mercy, a mediator of God's unfathomable mercy, so also, St. Faustina understood Mary to have an important role in her life, and in the life of the Church, as Mediatrix. Regardless of the fact that St. Faustina never referred to Mary using the title "Mediatrix,"[194] she nevertheless presents a clear picture of Mary's role as one who mediates and intercedes for God's people.

At one point in her early religious life, Jesus gave St. Faustina the following instructions when He wanted her to make a novena of holy hours: "During this adoration try to unite yourself in prayer with My Mother. Pray with all your heart in union with Mary ... ."[195] On another occasion, Jesus even instructed her to "ask My Mother and the saints for help."[196] Saint Faustina not only observed these injunctions of Jesus but did so throughout the entire duration of her life. In so many ways, St. Faustina used language that portrayed her understanding of Mary as a mediator and intercessor.

As has already been stated, though St. Faustina did not employ the terminology of "Mediatrix," this in no way implies that she did not see Mary as a maternal mediator. On the contrary, her frequent use of such mediation terminology portrays a clear understanding that Mary is both a maternal mediator and intercessor. This understanding of Mary as a maternal mediator is given through the following terminology that St. Faustina used in reference to Mary:

---

[194] Cf. *Lumen Gentium*, 62.

[195] *Diary*, 32.

[196] Ibid., 1560.

pray to,[197] *grant me the grace of,*[198] *I asked the Mother of God for graces,*[199] *She did not refuse any of my requests,*[200] *I begged her,*[201] *Your lives must be like Mine [Mary's] ... pleading for humanity,*[202] *unite me with Jesus, unite my soul to Jesus,*[203] *I entreat her,*[204] *help me attain,*[206] As well as all these examples that clearly manifest Mary's intercessory role, St. Faustina also made novenas *to* the Virgin Mary on numerous occasions, asking her intercession and mediation for a particular need.[207] Yet, there are even more explicit statements from St. Faustina's *Diary* that reveal a deep theological understanding of Mary's role as Mediatrix.

On one occasion when she was making a novena for her native Poland, St. Faustina recounted the following vision of Marian mediation:

> On the seventh day of the novena I saw, between heaven and earth, the Mother of God, clothed in a bright robe. She was praying with Her hands folded on Her bosom, Her eyes fixed on Heaven. From Her Heart issued forth fiery rays, some of which were turned toward Heaven while others were covering our country.[208]

The terminology of Mary being "between heaven and earth" gives evidence to Mary's maternal mediation in relation to her spiritual children. Also of significance is the fact that the rays coming from her heart seem to penetrate both into heaven

---

[197] See *Diary*, 1174.

[198] See *Diary*, 79.

[199] See *Diary*, 182.

[200] See *Diary*, 260.

[201] See *Diary*, 346.

[202] See *Diary*, 625.

[203] See *Diary*, 162.

[204] See *Diary*, 915.

[205] See *Diary*, 1114.

[206] See *Diary*, 1306.

[207] See *Diary*, 330, 1206.

[208] *Diary*, 33.

and down to earth, thus making of her heart a channel of graces, a point of mediation. Obviously, Mary is not the source of grace but rather, as spiritual mother, a mediator of grace.

Another important presentation of Marian mediation in the *Diary* can be seen when we look at her employment of the preposition "through." For example, in the year 1929, St. Faustina noted the following: "O Mary, You are joy, because through You God descended to earth [and] into my heart."[209] Saint Faustina was aware that without Mary she would not have Mercy Incarnate. In this sense, St. Faustina's understanding of Marian mediation is in accord with the notion of "to Jesus through Mary" used by St. Louis Marie de Montfort.[210] However, the most significant use of the preposition "through" comes in a poetic litany of Marian mediation written by St. Faustina in 1938:

> To give worthy praise to the Lord's mercy,
> We unite ourselves with Your Immaculate Mother,
> For then our hymn will be more pleasing to You,
> Because She is chosen from among men and angels.
>
> Through Her, as through a pure crystal, Your mercy was passed on to us. Through Her, man became pleasing to God. Through Her, streams of grace flowed down upon us.[211]

This litany of Marian mediation is theologically rich. Perhaps the most important theme is that Mary mediates mercy to us, that is, both Mercy Incarnate (the Divine Person of Jesus Christ), and the mercies (graces) of His redemption. As we have already seen, St. Faustina does understand Mary to be a maternal mediator of grace.[212] Truly, St. Faustina's use of the preposition "through" is a clear sign of her understanding of Marian mediation.

---

[209] *Diary*, 40.

[210] See St. Louis Marie de Montfort, *True Devotion to the Blessed Virgin* (Bay Shore, NY: Montfort Publications, 1996).

[211] *Diary*, 1746.

[212] See *Diary*, 182, 315.

Concerning the element of Marian intercession, St. Faustina also makes explicit reference to this role of Mary. For example, on several occasions she notes that through the intercession of Mary she obtained the graces of fidelity,[213] the belt of purity,[214] and an interior life.[215] On two occasions, St. Faustina even made use of the word "intercession" to describe Mary's maternal role:

> Most merciful Jesus, I beseech You through the intercession of Your Saints, and especially the intercession of Your dearest Mother who nurtured You from childhood, bless my native land.[216]

What is interesting in the above excerpt is the apparent appeal that St. Faustina is making to the maternity of Mary as a means of obtaining the blessing of Jesus — this resembles the *ostentatio mammarum* in the Marian tradition. The following excerpt also reveals the maternal intercession of Mary:

> I saw the Lord Jesus, like a king in great majesty, looking down upon our earth with great severity; but because of His Mother's intercession He prolonged the time of His mercy.[217]

Some might think the above passage medieval in its presentation of God being the just judge and Mary being the merciful mother, but this is to miss the point due to the fact that Mary has her role of maternal intercessor from the merciful Savior. Mary, of herself, can do nothing. Mary is able to intercede and prolong the time of mercy only because God desires it, willing her to be both Mother of Mercy and Mediatrix of Mercy.

---

[213] See *Diary*, 170.

[214] See *Diary*, 40.

[215] See *Diary*, 785.

[216] *Diary*, 286. Interestingly, as a further sign of her deep understanding of the need of mediation and intercession, she even asks certain saints to intercede for her before Jesus *and* Mary: "I have chosen Saint Claude de la Colombiere and Saint Gertrude as my patron saints for this retreat [Krakow, October 1936], that they may intercede for me before the Mother of God and the merciful Savior." See *Diary*, 728.

[217] *Diary*, 1261.

MOTHER OF MERCY

Mary's title of being Mother of Mercy is an ancient one.[218] In the *Diary*, St. Faustina used the title Mother of Mercy only one time, in a vision where Mary addresses St. Faustina's confessor: "I am not only the Queen of Heaven, but also the Mother of Mercy and your Mother."[219] This one-time-usage should not lead us to minimize the importance of this title in the life of St. Faustina. On the contrary, there are many indications within the *Diary* that St. Faustina had a deep understanding of this role of Mary.[220]

On at least two occasions, St. Faustina noted that she had experiences with Mary on the Congregation's patronal feast of Aug. 5.[221] On one of these occasions, Aug. 5, 1935, St. Faustina recorded Mary as telling her that her role as Mother is due to the mercy of God: "I am Mother to you all, thanks to the unfathomable mercy of God."[222] In addition, from a liturgical standpoint, the Ostra Brama image of Mary in Vilnius celebrates its feast as Our Lady of Mercy on Nov. 16, and St. Faustina often participated in this celebration.[223]

In addition to the *ostentatio mammarum* vision that conveys Mary's role as maternal intercessor of the mercy of God,[224] one of the most intriguing aspects of St. Faustina's notion of Mary as Mother of Mercy comes from her frequent reference to Mary's mantle serving as a refuge of

---

[218] This title was first used by St. Odo of Cluny in the 10th century. See St. Odo of Cluny, *Vita Odonis*, I, 9: PL 133, 47b, 72.

[219] *Diary*, 330.

[220] On the patronal feast of the Congregation, Our Lady of the Snows, the Sisters celebrate the Feast of Our Lady of Mercy, and on August 5, 1937 the community elected Mary to be the Superior General of the Congregation. The "Act of Election of the Mother of Mercy as Superior General of the Congregation" can be found in the appendix. St. Faustina lived through these events and relates them in *Diary* entry 1244.

[221] See *Diary*, 266, 449.

[222] *Diary*, 449.

[223] See *Diary*, 529.

[224] See *Diary*, 686.

mercy.[225] There are a total of seven times where St. Faustina uses this imagery to capture Mary's role as Mother of Mercy. The specific citations are the following:

"O my Mother, cover my soul with Your virginal mantle. ..."[226]

"O Mary, my Mother, I humbly beg of You, cover my soul with Your virginal cloak. ..."[227]

"And at that moment She stretched out her right hand, in which She was clasping Her mantle, and She covered the priest with it."[228]

"She approached me from the altar, touched me with Her hands and covered me with Her mantle. ..."[229]

"Suddenly, I saw the Blessed Mother, who shielded him [her confessor] with Her cloak. ..."[230]

"Since that time [of receiving the belt of purity], I have been living under the virginal cloak of the Mother of God."[231]

"And at that moment [at the end of the liturgical celebration on August 15, 1937, in which Mary, as Mother of Mercy, was solemnly celebrated as their Superior General] She covered all the sisters of our Congregation with Her mantle. With her right hand,

---

[225] Mary's maternal mantle serving as a mantle of protection and mercy from the Mother of Mercy has often been depicted in Christian art, and can be seen in the following works: Enguerrand Quarton, *La Vierge de Miséricorde* (c.1453) France: Chateau musée Condé; Piero Della Francesca, *La Madonna della Misericordia* (c.1445) Borgo Sansepolcro: Museo Civico. Furthermore, the Order of Our Lady of Ransom (Mercedarians) founded in the 13th century have often presented Mary's mantle as a refuge of mercy.

[226] *Diary*, 79.

[227] Ibid., 220.

[228] Ibid., 330.

[229] Ibid., 468.

[230] Ibid., 597.

[231] Ibid., 1097.

She clasped Mother General Michael to herself, and with Her left hand She did so to me, while all the sisters were at Her feet, covered with Her mantle."[232]

These passages reveal that St. Faustina, especially in relation to the virtue of purity, sought refuge under the mantle of the Mother of Mercy. Living under the refuge of Mary's mantle of mercy was for St. Faustina a visual way of describing her love for Mary under the title of the Mother of Mercy, and of showing her filial relationship in regard to Mary's spiritual motherhood.[233]

One other thing that should be noted regarding St. Faustina's seeking refuge in mercy is a prayer she wrote in the final year of her life. Although this prayer is addressed to God and does not have a reference to Mary, it nonetheless seems to be a melding of the two Marian prayers known as the *Sub Tuum Praesidium* and the *Memorare*. It reads:

> I fly to Your mercy, Compassionate God, who alone are good. Although my misery is great, and my offenses are many, I trust in Your mercy, because You are the God of mercy; and, from time imme-morial, it has never been heard of, nor do heaven and earth remember, that a soul trusting in Your mercy has been disappointed.[234]

The *Sub Tuum Praesidium* (c. 3ʳᵈ century) may be trans-lated as follows:

> Under your mercy, we take refuge, Mother of God, do not reject our supplications in necessity. But deliver us from danger. [You] alone chaste, alone blessed.[235]

---

[232] Ibid., 1244.

[233] St. Faustina's notion of a cloak being a refuge of mercy is even evidenced in her relationship with the merciful Savior: "You have covered me with the cloak of Your mercy, pardoning my sins." See *Diary*, 1489.

[234] *Diary*, 1730.

[235] G. Giamberardini, "Il 'Sub tuum praesidium' e il titolo 'Theotokos' nella tradizione egiziana," *Marianum 31* (1969), 348.

The *Memorare*, traditionally attributed to St. Bernard of Clairvaux, reads:

Remember, O most gracious Virgin Mary, that never was it known that anyone who fled to your protection, implored your help or sought your intercession, was left unaided. Inspired with this confidence, I fly to you, O Virgin of virgins, my Mother; to you do I come, before you I stand, sinful and sorrowful. O Mother of the Word Incarnate, despise not my petitions, but in your mercy hear and answer me.[236]

MEDIATRIX OF MERCY

Mary's role as Mother of Mercy also brings out her role as Mediatrix of Mercy.[237] St. Faustina, though never explicitly calling Mary "Mediatrix of Mercy," understood that due to the maternal role of Mary in salvation, God desired Mary to mediate mercy to us — both mercy understood as the Incarnation of the Second Person of the Trinity and as the graces flowing from the redemption. That Mary has been understood to be a Mediatrix of Mercy is a long-standing tradition in the Church, often associated with her Divine Maternity, spiritual motherhood, and Queenship. Concerning this, Pope Leo XIII offered a glimpse of this tradition in his 1891 encyclical on the Rosary, *Octobri Mense*:

... may it also be affirmed that, by the will of God, Mary is the intermediary through whom is distributed unto us this immense treasure of mercies gathered by God, for mercy and truth were created by Jesus Christ. Thus as no man goeth to the Father but by the Son, so no man goeth to Christ but by His Mother. How great are the goodness

---

[236] *Dictionary of Mary*, (New Jersey: Catholic Book Publishing Co., 1997), 324.

[237] As already noted, Mary's role of mediation follows her role as spiritual mother. Thus, there is a distinction between the title Mother of Mercy (a title conveying "being") and the title Mediatrix of Mercy (a title conveying action).

and mercy revealed in this design of God![238]

In the terminology of St. Faustina, the Incarnation of the Word is a 'miracle of mercy' that comes through the Immaculate womb of Mary.[239] In this sense Mary is Mediatrix of Mercy Incarnate. Yet, as in the following statement — "through Her [Mary], as through a pure crystal, Your mercy was passed on to us"[240] — St. Faustina understood Mary's role as Mediatrix of Mercy to extend to individual graces given to the sinner, graces that come in the form of mercy. Indeed, it includes each individual grace that comes to us in the form of mercy, because everything *ad extra* the Trinity has the stamp of mercy.

Further examples of how St. Faustina portrayed Mary as fulfilling her role as Mediatrix of Mercy can be seen in the passages where she saw Mary interceding for the poor souls in purgatory as "Star of the Sea,"[241] and in her presentation of Mary prolonging the time of mercy because of her maternal intercessions.[242] Both of these examples display that Mary exercises her maternal role in relation to souls in the form of mediating the mercies of Christ to those in need.

VIRGINITY

The theme of the virginity of Mary is also prominent in the *Diary* of St. Faustina. Since St. Faustina was not an academic theologian but a mystical theologian, her various presentations of Mary's virginity are not put in the doctrinal

---

[238] Pope Leo XIII, *Octobri Mense,* 4.

[239] See *Diary,* 1745.

[240] *Diary,* 1746.

[241] See *Diary,* 20.

[242] See *Diary,* 1261.

formulas that make up this particular teaching of the Church, namely, virginity before birth (*virginitas ante partum*), virginity in birth (*virginitas in partu*) and virginity after birth (*virginitas post partum*). However, in the many visions that St. Faustina had of the Mother of God, she does often call Mary "Virgin" in situations where it is apparent that Mary is understood to be a virgin before birth (e.g., Advent visions and references to Mary's pregnancy),[243] during birth (a vision on Christmas day),[244] and after the birth of Christ (Presentation in the Temple).[245] All in all, each within a particular context, St. Faustina refers to Mary as "virgin" a total of 29 times.[246]

As descriptive ways of presenting Mary's virginity, St. Faustina often referred to Mary's virginity as "immaculate"[247] and "radiant."[248] However, one of the most interesting facets of her presentation of the virginity of Mary is in her classification of three specific aspects that are important in understanding the virginity of Mary: her "virginal heart,"[249] her "virginal womb,"[250] and her "virginal mantle."[251] In a certain sense, these three distinct dimensions of Mary's virginity refer to her virginity as interior (heart), exterior (womb/body), and as a part of her spiritual motherhood exercised towards mankind (mantle).

---

[243] See *Diary*, 161, 844, 1746.

[244] See *Diary*, 1442.

[245] See *Diary*, 915. As has already been noted, in two of the four encounters that St. Faustina had with St. Joseph, she presents him as being an "Old Man". See *Diary*, 608, 846. In addition, during a vision in which she is present at the birth of Christ, neither St. Joseph nor St. Faustina are able to see the birth of Christ, and this is, most likely, due to the wonder of the virgin birth. See *Diary*, 1442.

[246] See *Diary*, 40, 93, 161, 309, 449, 454, 843-844, 874, 915, 1232-1233, 1244, 1251, 1300, 1306, 1410, 1413, 1442, 1711, 1742, 1745-1746.

[247] See *Diary*, 843, 874, 1232, 1413.

[248] See *Diary*, 844.

[249] See *Diary*, 161.

[250] See *Diary*, 1746.

[251] See *Diary*, 79, 220, 1097.

IMMACULATE CONCEPTION

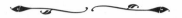

The time in which St. Faustina lived was an intensely Marian period in Church history, especially in regard to the Immaculate Conception. In the previous century, Blessed Pope Pius IX had dogmatically defined Mary's Immaculate Conception (*Ineffabilis Deus*) and one year before St. Faustina's birth, St. Pius X wrote an encyclical to commemorate the fiftieth anniversary of the dogma (*Ad Diem Illum*). In addition, the Marian apparitions to St. Bernadette Soubirous in Lourdes, France, in 1858 and the profound writings and founding in 1917 of the *Militia Immaculatae* of Poland's native son, St. Maximilian Maria Kolbe, are further evidence of this era of the Immaculate Conception. Regarding the Lourdes connection, it is interesting to note that in 1907 the Holy See established the Feast of Our Lady of Lourdes, and that the image so often depicted as the Immaculate Conception, namely, Mary wearing a white dress with a blue sash, was often how Mary appeared to St. Faustina.[252]

Many of the doctrinal aspects that St. Faustina underscored in her various statements on the Immaculate Conception offer an echo of the teaching of the Church on this privilege of Our Lady. For example, in the mind of St. Faustina, the Immaculate Conception serves as a "sturdy anchor," "shield," "protection," and "strength."[253] By using these descriptive words, St. Faustina shows the understanding of the Church that the Immaculate Conception points to Christ and assures us of His love and desire to save us — in this sense, the Immaculate Conception gives us hope.

Saint Faustina also echoed the Church's teaching that it

---

[252] See *Diary,* 468 (Feast of the Assumption), 564 (Feast of the Immaculate Conception), 805 (Feast of the Immaculate Conception).

[253] See *Diary,* 161, 1232.

is because of Mary's Immaculate Conception that she can be both Virgin and Mother. The Immaculate Conception allows Mary to be "without blemish" and "beyond all comparison."[254] She even presents the person of the Immaculate Conception as being "ever untouched by sin,"[255] implying that the Immaculate Conception, both as *event* and as *person*, is without sin, that is, she has neither original nor personal sin. This is why St. Faustina used the terminology that the Immaculate Conception is a "unique privilege,"[256] not a privilege that separates Mary from us, but a privilege that unites Mary ever so closely to all humanity. Knowing that this privilege accorded to Mary was intended by God to draw us closer to Himself, St. Faustina was not remiss in thanking the Trinity for this privilege, and this gratitude brought great joy to Mary.[257]

Furthermore, in addition to St. Faustina's notion that the Immaculate Conception was willed "from all ages,"[258] which could be a reference to understanding a certain absolute primacy with regard to the Immaculate Conception, St. Faustina also goes beyond the average presentation of the Immaculate Conception with her notion that it is a mystery of light and a gift intimately associated with The Divine Mercy.

Concerning the issue of the Immaculate Conception being a mystery of light, there are numerous occasions in the *Diary* where St. Faustina makes a correlation between the two. The following excerpts make this connection clear:

> You [Immaculate Virgin] are beautiful as the sun ...[259]

> On the feast day of the Immaculate Conception ... I heard the rustling of garments and saw the most Holy Mother of God in a most beautiful radiance.[260]

---

[254] See *Diary*, 161.

[255] *Diary*, 1746.

[256] See *Diary*, 1412.

[257] See *Diary*, 564, 1412.

[258] See *Diary*, 1746.

[259] *Diary*, 161.

[260] Ibid., 564.

[On the feast of the Immaculate Conception]
Marvelous light streamed forth from Her whole
figure.[261]

[On the feast of the Immaculate Conception] I saw
a certain priest who was surrounded by the light
which flowed from Her; evidently, this soul loves
the Immaculate One.[262]

O Mother, Immaculate Virgin, in You the divine
ray is reflected. ...[263]

Mary's person is at one and the same time a presence
that radiates light as well as a reflection of the greater light of
God.

Although she does not go into detail and precise theological explanations, perhaps St. Faustina's most insightful
doctrinal element in her understanding of the Immaculate
Conception is that it is a mystery of mercy. As the Immaculate
Conception, Mary "is first to praise the omnipotence of Your
[God's] mercy."[264] While this is certainly an allusion to Mary's
praise of God's mercy in the Magnificat (see Lk. 1:50, 54), it
can also refer to the fact that as the Immaculate Conception,
the perfect fruit flowing from the redemption of Christ, she is
the masterpiece of Divine Mercy.

Most likely, St. Faustina would completely understand
the profound statements made by John Paul II concerning
Mary and the mystery of mercy: "Mary ... is the one who *has
the deepest knowledge of the mystery of God's mercy,*" and who
has "*obtained mercy in an exceptional way.*"[265] What St.
Faustina formulated in a simple poetic phrase theologians
have come to understand as a crucial Mariological truth,
namely, Mary, especially in the mystery of her Immaculate

---

[261] Ibid., 805.

[262] Ibid., 806.

[263] Ibid., 1232.

[264] Ibid., 1746.

[265] John Paul II, *Dives in Misericordia,* 9.

Conception, is the masterpiece of Divine Mercy.[266] Thus, the intimate connection between Divine Mercy and the Immaculate Conception makes St. Faustina's favored Marian privilege, the Immaculate Conception, all the more understandable: The Immaculate Conception is pure mercy. For this reason, just as St. Faustina spent all of her energy in promoting Divine Mercy, we also note her saying that "nothing is too much when it comes to honoring the Immaculate Virgin."[267]

In many of the instances where St. Faustina wrote about Mary's Immaculate Conception, she also seemed to insinuate that by coming in contact with this great mystery, the person is drawn into the mystery of purity. In a certain sense, Mary's Immaculate Conception seems to work in a causal way in helping a person become pure, not as an efficient cause, of course, but as an instrumental cause. The Immaculate Conception, in the mind of St. Faustina, seems to be something like the pattern of purity that souls are to imitate and after which they should strive.

This "causal" dimension of the Immaculate Conception is seen in 1936 when St. Faustina mentioned on the Feast of the Immaculate Conception the following: "From today onwards, I am going to strive for the greatest purity of soul, that the rays of God's grace may be reflected in all their brilliance. I long to be a crystal in order to find favor in His eyes."[268] As we will see in the next chapter, St. Faustina both calls Mary a pure crystal reflecting the rays of God, and expresses her strong and ardent desire to become like Mary, that is, a pure crystal reflecting God's brilliance. The imitation of the Immaculate is extremely important for St. Faustina.

Another excerpt points to a correlation between Mary Immaculate and obtaining and preserving the virtue of purity: "Mary, Immaculate Virgin, take me under Your special protection and guard the purity of my soul, heart and body.

---

[266] Cf. Fr. Marie-Dominique Philippe, OP, *Mary, Mystery of Mercy.* (Stockbridge, MA: Marian Press, 2002), esp., pp.17-51.

[267] *Diary*, 1413.

[268] *Diary*, 805.

You are the model and star of my life."[269] Once again, Mary's state of being Immaculate serves as a protection, guard, model, star, light, and guide in matters concerning purity.

ASSUMPTION

In addition to the Feast of the Immaculate Conception, it seems that the Feast of the Assumption of Mary into heaven occupied a special place in the spiritual life of St. Faustina. While her writings on the Assumption do not offer any insights concerning doctrinal matters, of all the Marian feasts she mentions from the time she began re-writing her *Diary* in 1934, the feast of the Assumption is the only one that is mentioned every year (1934, 1935, 1936, 1937). The Feast of the Immaculate Conception, though treated in a deeper way, is only mentioned three times (1935, 1936, 1937).

From an artistic standpoint, on each of the four occasions where St. Faustina saw Mary on the Feast of the Assumption,[270] she wrote about the unspeakable beauty of Mary. Furthermore, in two of these accounts she notes that Mary is assumed into heaven with an uncovered head and flowing hair.[271] This is interesting from an artistic perspective because many artists have traditionally depicted Mary assumed into heaven with uncovered head and flowing hair as a way of showing her virginal purity and beauty.[272]

---

[269] Ibid., 874.

[270] See *Diary,* 325, 468, 677, 1243.

[271] See *Diary,* 468, 677.

[272] Examples of art depicting Mary being assumed into heaven with uncovered head and flowing hair can be seen in the following: Michel Sittow (1469-1525), *The Assumption of the Virgin* (c.1500), Washington, D.C.: National Gallery of Art; El Greco [Domenico Theotocopuli] (1541-1614), *The Assumption of the Virgin* (c.1577), Chicago: Art Institute of Chicago; Nicolas Poussin (1594-1665), *The Assumption of the Virgin* (c.1626), Washington, D.C.: National Gallery of Art;

QUEENSHIP

In the *Diary* St. Faustina referred to Mary as a Queen twice,[273] though she never made mention of the Feast of the Queenship of Mary.[274] Neither does she refer to Our Lady as the Queen of Poland, a title dear to the heart of the Polish people. In the two passages where Mary presents herself as a Queen, she also makes reference to her spiritual motherhood, even putting it above her role as Queen. This is significant from a doctrinal point of view because it relates the truth that Mary is only Queen because of her maternal roles (Divine and Spiritual Motherhood) in the economy of salvation. In other words, her royal role of Queen is dependent upon her maternal role. This should not lead us to downplay her royal role as Queen, however. On the contrary, St. Faustina fully recognized the truth of Mary's royal dignity, as is depicted in the following descriptive account:

> A vision of the Mother of God. In the midst of a great brilliance, I saw the Mother of God clothed in a white gown, girt about with a golden cincture; and there were tiny stars, also of gold, over the whole garment, and chevron-shaped sleeves lined with gold. Her cloak was sky-blue, lightly thrown over the shoulders. A transparent veil was delicately drawn over her head, while her flowing hair was set off beautifully by a golden crown which terminated in little crosses.[275]

Bartolome Murillo (1617-1682), *The Assumption of the Virgin* (c. 1670), The Hermitage Museum: St. Petersburg.

[273] See *Diary,* 330, 805.

[274] In the old liturgical calendar the Feast of Mary's Queenship was celebrated on May 31st. Now May 31st is celebrated as the Feast of the Visitation of Mary, and the Queenship has been moved to August 22nd.

[275] *Diary,* 1585.

This vision certainly conveys Mary's royal person and yet, at the same time, it is the vision where Mary identifies herself as the Mother of God of priests, thus identifying herself, in both visual presentation and verbal communication, as the Queen-Mother. As Queen-Mother, Mary is understood to be the dispenser of the mercies of Jesus Christ the King.[276]

---

[276] Cf. Urban Mullaney, OP, "The Coronation: Queen of Mercy," *Alma Socia Christi: Acta Congressus Mariologici-Mariani Romae anno Sancto MCML Celebrati. Vol.III: De Praedistinatione et regalitate B. Virginis Mariae.* (Romae: Academia Mariana, 1952): 93-110.

CHAPTER IV

Marian Devotion in
St. Faustina's Spirituality

T he word "devotion" appears four times in St. Faustina's *Diary* when referring to her relationship with the Blessed Virgin.[277] It is a word that refers to one person who has a love for another person, a love that stems from affection and the will. Concerning this, Sr. Elzbieta Siepak rightly notes the following: "Sister Faustina's relationship with the Most Blessed Mother was extremely loving and close, based on the great intimacy that can only exist between the tenderest Mother and Her loving daughter."[278] Though St. Faustina only used the word "devotion" four times, examples of Marian devotion are replete in her *Diary*.

As a young girl St. Faustina already had a tremendous devotion to the Mother of God. Her entrance into religious life most certainly enhanced and added new fervor to her Marian devotion. The aim of this chapter is to present and analyze the various examples of Marian devotion practiced by St. Faustina, a person so in love with the Virgin Mary that she could spend six hours in front of the Czestochowa image lost in prayer,[279] and state that devotion to the Mother of God makes one a true child of God.[280]

As is the case in the lives of the saints, there are certain elements in St. Faustina's Marian devotion that are to be expected, for example, her love of the Rosary, the Immaculate Heart, Marian novenas, the sorrows of Mary, and consecration prayers to the Mother of God, which will be covered later. However, some of the more particular aspects of St. Faustina's Marian devotion will center on her manner of expression when describing her Marian devotion (poetic praises) and her use of various metaphors (flowers, crystal, shield). As a whole, these elements will give clear evidence that St. Faustina can truly be said to have been thoroughly devoted to Our Lady.

---

[277] See *Diary,* 40, 93, 1388, 1704.

[278] *SSF,* 91.

[279] See *Diary,* 260.

[280] See *Diary,* 1388.

POETIC PRAISE OF THE VIRGIN MARY

The styles of certain aspects of St. Faustina's Marian entries in her *Diary* are written in a literary, poetic way. In a certain sense, most of these instances cannot be considered a hard and fast application of the principles of poetry, which are, observing the conventions of measure and form. Nevertheless, the fact that she wrote over 30 poetry-style sections, of which three are Marian, gives clear indication that her spirituality was often expressed using the mystical category of poetry. Unfortunately, the Polish original loses something of the elegance and fluidity of the particular piece when translated into English.

Perhaps the best terminology for describing the style in which St. Faustina wrote her poetry, whether to Mary, Jesus or a spiritual theme, is to label it *poetic praise*. This means that St. Faustina desired to express both her devotion and praise (wonder) to the theme being presented in the format of a religious poem. Most all of her poems contain an element of intense fascination with the topic being put into poetry. Indeed, her poetic praises reflect the depths of a mystic caught up in deep contemplation of the mystery before her.

To more fully understand St. Faustina's intense devotion to the Mother of God as expressed in her poetic praises, let us examine all three of her Marian poems.[281]

Marian Poem #1: Purest of All Lilies

O Mary, Immaculate Virgin,
Pure crystal for my heart,
You are my strength, O sturdy anchor!
You are the weak heart's shield and protection.

---

[281] The titles provided for the three Marian poems are my own.

O Mary you are pure, of purity incomparable;
At once both Virgin and Mother,
You are beautiful as the sun, without blemish,
And Your soul is beyond all comparison.

Your beauty has delighted the eye of the Thrice-Holy
    One.
He descended from heaven, leaving His eternal throne,
And took Body and Blood of Your heart
And for nine months lay hidden in a Virgin's Heart.

O Mother, Virgin, purest of all lilies,
Your heart was Jesus' first tabernacle on earth.
Only because no humility was deeper than Yours
Were You raised above the choirs of Angels and
    above all Saints.
O Mary, my sweet Mother,
I give You my soul, my body and my poor heart.
Be the guardian of my life,
Especially at the hour of death, in the final strife.[282]

This poem deals explicitly with St. Faustina's love for
Mary Immaculate. Mary is described as all beautiful, pure,
without blemish and a lily. The poem begins and leads into
very descriptive statements about the wonder of Mary's
holiness, and ends with a form of consecration to her.

Marian Poem #2: My Shield and Defense

O sweet Mother of God,
I model my life on You;
You are for me the bright dawn;
In You I lose myself, enraptured.

O Mother, Immaculate Virgin,
In You the divine ray is reflected,

---

[282] *Diary,* 161.

Midst storms, 'tis You who teach me to love the Lord,
O my shield and defense from the foe.[283]

This poetic praise of the Blessed Virgin contains strong
elements of Mary's exemplary nature and what has been clas-
sically titled the *imitatio Mariae*. Mary is worthy of imitation
because of her close relationship to God and to mankind. In
relation to God she serves as a reflection, in relation to man
she serves as a Mother and shield.

Marian Poem #3: Snow-White Lily

Be adored, O God of mercy,
Because You have deigned to descend from heaven
    to earth.
Most humbly we adore You
For Your having vouchsafed to exalt all mankind.
Unfathomable and incomprehensible in Your mercy,
For love of us You take on flesh
From the Immaculate Virgin, ever untouched by sin,
Because You have willed it so from all ages.

The Blessed Virgin, that Snow-White Lily,
Is first to praise the omnipotence of Your mercy.
Her pure heart opens with love for the coming of
    the Word;
She believes the words of God's messenger and is
    confirmed in trust.

Heaven is astounded that God has become man,
That there is on earth a heart worthy of God Himself.
Why is it that You do not unite Yourself with a Seraph,
    but with a sinner, O Lord?
Oh, because, despite the purity of the virginal womb,
This is a mystery of Your mercy.

[283] Ibid., 1232

O mystery of God's mercy, O God of compassion,
That You have deigned to leave the heavenly throne
And to stoop down to our misery, to human weakness,
For it is not the angels, but man who needs mercy.

To give worthy praise to the Lord's mercy,
We unite ourselves with Your Immaculate Mother,
For then our hymn will be more pleasing to You,
Because She is chosen from among men and angels.

Through Her, as through a pure crystal,
Your mercy was passed on to us.
Through Her, man became pleasing to God;
Through Her, streams of grace flowed down
   upon us.[284]

This poetic praise centers on the dual themes of Mary and Divine Mercy. St. Faustina draws out the existing mingling between these two mysteries, even focusing at the end on the mediation of Mary in regard to mercy. Furthermore, Mary's intimate participation in the Incarnation is seen as a great wonder worthy of the highest praise and honor.

METAPHORS

Another way that St. Faustina described the wonder of Mary was through the use of metaphors. Since devotion comes from the heart and is often difficult to describe, mystics often times employ metaphors in order to try to express a deep truth inherent in their particular spirituality or devotion. In this, St. Faustina is no different.

---

[284] Ibid., 1746

There are many symbols and metaphors that St. Faustina used to describe Mary. Many of these are common in the Mariological tradition. However, there are a few metaphors that St. Faustina seemed to favor over others, for example, flowers (especially the lily), crystal imagery, and Mary as a shield. Naturally, when St. Faustina uses these metaphors to speak of Mary, she is trying to develop a particular aspect of how she understood both Mary in relation to God and Mary in relation to us. For this reason, the metaphors of devotion reveal great insights into St. Faustina's love for Mary.

FLOWERS

The association of flowers with certain dimensions of the spiritual life has been a constant theme throughout the Judeo-Christian tradition. In fact, when considering the Virgin Mary and her place in the spiritual life, it makes perfect sense that flowers often have been named after her and used as metaphors for understanding her maternal role and the devotion due to her. One only has to think of that most beautiful of prayers, the Rosary.[285] Fr. Lucius McClean, in the introduction to the book by Mabel Maugham (Beldy), *Our Lady's Flowers,* notes the following concerning the connection between Mary and flowers:

> From the earliest Christian times, flowers have been associated with Our Lady. The Liturgy constantly stresses this association, and Christ's people have been long used to calling Mary by such names as "The Lily of the Valley," and "Mystical Rose." Flowers symbolizing virtues like modesty, humility, purity, love, have been, as it were, dedicated to her.[286]

Before delving into St. Faustina's particular use of floral images in describing Mary, it is important to note the overall

---

[285] Cf. Louis Gemminger, *Flowers of Mary.* (Baltimore: John Murphy & Co., 1894).

[286] Lucius McClean, in Mabel Maugham (Beldy), *Our Lady's Flowers.* (Dublin: Assisi Press, 1958), 3.

application that St. Faustina gave to flowers in her spiritual writing. She will often times describe herself as a flower in order to highlight some particular aspect of her spiritual life. For example, she seemed to have understood certain kinds of flowers as representing various aspects of the spiritual life: humility = violet, love = rose, purity (and suffering) = lily. Of these three, the lily was St. Faustina's favorite flower. Therefore, this section, while briefly presenting St. Faustina's metaphorical use of the violet and the rose, will focus primarily upon her fascination with the lily.

Concerning humility, St. Faustina gave clear statements that humility is a lovely flower,[287] and the following examples show how she associated this virtue with the violet:

> I will hide myself among the sisters like a little violet among lilies. I want to blossom for my Lord and Maker, to forget about myself, to empty myself totally for the sake of immortal souls.[288]

> I want to be a tiny violet, hidden in the grass, unknown in a magnificent enclosed garden in which beautiful lilies and roses grow. The beautiful rose and the lovely lily can be seen from afar, but in order to see a little violet, one has to bend low; only its scent gives it away.[289]

> I will hide from people's eyes whatever good I am able to do so that God Himself may be my reward. I will be like a tiny violet hidden in the grass, which does not hurt the foot that treads on it, but diffuses its fragrance and, forgetting itself completely, tries to please the person who has crushed it underfoot.[290]

Concerning love, St. Faustina associated this virtue with both a rose and her very own heart, often times described as

---

[287] See *Diary*, 275, 296, 306, 1306.

[288] *Diary*, 224.

[289] Ibid., 591.

[290] Ibid., 255.

a beautiful garden. For example, in her *Diary*, we read the following passages:

> O my divine Bridegroom, the flower of my heart and the scent of my pure love are for You.[291]

> Jesus, behold my heart which is for You a dwelling place to which no one else has entry. You alone repose in it as in a beautiful garden.[292]

> I cast myself as a little rosebud at Your feet, O Lord, and may the fragrance of this flower be known to You alone.[293]

> I want to live pure as a wild flower; I want my love always to be turned to You, just as a flower that is always turning to the sun. I want the fragrance and the freshness of the flower of my heart to be always presevered for You alone.[294]

> Under the influence of His rays, my soul has become covered with verdure, flowers, and fruit, and has become a beautiful garden for His repose.[295]

> O my most sweet Master, good Jesus, I give You my heart. You shape and mold it after Your liking. O fathomless love, I open the calyx of my heart to You, like a rosebud to the freshness of dew. To You alone, my Betrothed, is known the fragrance of the flower of my heart.[296]

The above examples of the metaphor of her love being like a rose manifest the depths of St. Faustina's heartfelt devotion to Christ. As a matter of fact, Christ Himself noted

---

[291] Ibid., 591.

[292] Ibid., 1385.

[293] Ibid., 239.

[294] Ibid., 306.

[295] Ibid., 605.

[296] Ibid., 1064.

to her on two occasions that He took delight in her heart as in a "rosebud at morningtide"[297] and a "garden enclosed."[298] Concerning the virtue of purity, St. Faustina most definitely understood this to be imaged in the metaphor of the lily. However, what is perhaps most interesting is the fact that St. Faustina never *explicitly* called herself a lily. St. Faustina *infers*, as we will see in the next section, that she is a lily due to her virginity, but *explicitly* refers to Mary as a lily. Perhaps since she held purity to be so great in the spiritual life, she only refers to the love of Jesus and Mary as being lily-like.[299]

One of the most comprehensive applications of the metaphor of flowers can be seen in the following passage:

> My life is not drab or monotonous, but it is varied like a garden of fragrant flowers, so that I don't know which flower to pick first, the lily of suffering or the rose of love of neighbor or the violet of humility.[300]

It is interesting that on one occasion when Jesus desired to show His love for St. Faustina, He miraculously changed a pot of boiled potatoes into a pot of roses,[301] and, on the other hand, when Satan wanted to manifest his hatred for St. Faustina, he violently hurled a flowerpot to the ground, smashing it to pieces.[302]

The fact that at age five, St. Faustina had a dream in which she was walking hand in hand with the Mother of God in a beautiful garden proves to be significant when we examine how later in life St. Faustina used the metaphor of flowers to describe the Virgin Mary. St. Faustina's love and devotion to Mary was so intense during her life as a religious that she chose to describe Mary in terms that were familiar to

---

[297] See *Diary*, 1546.

[298] See *Diary*, 581.

[299] See, for example, *Diary* 1575 where she describes Jesus' love as "purer than a lily".

[300] *Diary*, 296.

[301] See *Diary*, 65.

[302] See *Diary*, 411-412.

herself. As a religious, St. Faustina had often been assigned to be the gardener in convents, and this gave her a familiarity with various flowers and their fragrances. In addition, in the month of May when flowers are in bloom, Marian devotions flourish in Poland; on one occasion, Faustina even noted that for her May devotions, she laid the flower of her silence at the feet of the Mother of God.[303]

In the history of Christianity, many scriptural verses,[304] theological writings,[305] and artists have used the lily as a metaphor for describing both the beauty and the purity of the Mother of God.[306] Concerning artistic presentations, Fr. Lucius McClean, notes the following:

> For the Old Masters [artists], plants and flowers proclaimed beliefs and dogmas of their faith. A lily in a pot in a picture of the Annunciation said that Mary's virginity remained intact even though she was becoming the Mother of God. A bower or spray of roses proclaimed what the Liturgy had already applied to her from Scripture, that she is the Mother of Fair Love. A bunch of grapes told the whole story of the Eucharist, of how the Precious Blood Christ had first taken from the virginal body of His Mother had been given for us on Calvary and to us in the Holy Communion.[307]

---

[303] See *Diary,* 1105.

[304] See, Song of Songs 2:2; Mt. 6:28-29.

[305] For example, the following quotes come from two Fathers of the Church: "Mary is the most beautiful lily in the garden of God, for her heart was never sullied by the least sin" St. Epiphanius, as quoted in Gemminger, *Flowers of Mary,* 32; "My Lady most holy, all-pure, all-immaculate, all-stainless, all-undefiled, all-incorrupt, all-inviolate immaculate robe of Him Who clothes Himself with light as with a garment . . . sweet-smelling rose, flower unfading, shining white lily, alone most immaculate" St. Ephrem the Syrian, *Oratio ad Deiparam in Enchiridion Marianum Biblicum Patristicum.* ed. D. Casagrande (Roma: Cor Unum, 1974), 341.

[306] Interestingly, even Bl. Pius IX in the Apostolic Constitution *Ineffabilis Deus,* which defined the dogma of the Immaculate Conception, noted: " . . . the Fathers [of the Church] have never ceased to call the Mother of God the lily among thorns, the land entirely intact, the Virgin undefiled, immaculate . . .".

[307] *OLF,* 4.

Further indication of the power of Christian art to transmit theological truths and devotion concerning the Mother of God through the employment of the theological metaphor of flowers is provided by Vincenzina Krymow:

> The lily was associated with the annunciation in Italian art early in the fourteenth century, especially in Florence, which had the lily as its emblem. During the fourteenth and fifteenth, centuries, the lily was sometimes depicted being carried by the archangel Gabriel. Later a vase of lilies, signifying Mary's purity, stood at her side. ... In the "Annunciation" attributed to Pietro di Giovanni Ambrosi, the angel holds three lily stalks to symbolize Mary's purity before, during and after the conception of her son.[308]

These historical facts are important to keep in mind when considering the application of the lily metaphor to Mary in the writings of St. Faustina. While St. Faustina did not paint an image of Our Lady, the devotional (and theological) aspect of how she related the lily to Mary remains the same.[309]

In the *Diary*, there are three specific times when St. Faustina referred to Mary as a lily. Each of these has a distinct context in which it is presented, but all share a similar theme. The passages are as follows:

> O my Mother, cover my soul with Your virginal mantle and grant me the grace of purity of heart, soul and body. ... O lovely lily! You are for me a mirror, O my Mother![310]

In the above passage, we note one of the constant themes of St. Faustina in regard to her Marian devotion,

---

[308] Vincenzina Krymow, *Mary's Flowers: Gardens, Legends & Meditations.* (Cincinnati: St. Anthony Messenger Press, 2002), 28.

[309] It should be noted that even in the secular world there is a specific kind of lily that has received the name "Madonna Lily" or *Lilium Candidum*. Cf. *OLF*, 2; *MFGLM*, 27-29.

[310] *Diary*, 79.

namely, the acquisition of and the perseverance in purity. Saint Faustina desired to see Mary's purity reflected in herself, thus the employment of the mirror metaphor. Saint Faustina also wanted to be a lily like Mary:

> O Mary you are pure, of purity incomparable;
> At once both Virgin and Mother,
> You are beautiful as the sun, without blemish,
> And Your soul is beyond all comparison. ...
> O Mother, Virgin, purest of all lilies,
> Your heart was Jesus' first tabernacle on earth.[311]

In this passage, there is both devotional and theological truth expressed in that Mary is pure (virginity) as a lily even in her motherhood (maternity), and deserves the devotional title of the "purest of all lilies." What Faustina is basically stating from a devotional perspective is that Mary is the "Virgin of Virgins." No other created human person has purity like Mary.

The last instance where St. Faustina employs the use of the lily metaphor to describe Mary occurs in her poem on Mary and the mystery of mercy:

> The Blessed Virgin, that Snow-White Lily, Is first to praise the omnipotence of Your mercy. Her pure heart opens with love for the coming of the Word. ...[312]

What this excerpt reveals is St. Faustina's use of the mixed metaphor of the lily and the heart. In essence, St. Faustina presents Mary's heart as being a repose, a calyx, opening to receive the Lord. This is, in fact, what St. Faustina herself desired to be. Mary's depiction as a lily, therefore, reveals that St. Faustina had a devotional understanding of Mary that was deeply grounded in the imitation of the virtues of Mary. What is striking about this, as we have seen, is that at no time does St. Faustina refer to herself as a lily. Most likely this is because she held Mary in such high regard that St. Faustina did not think herself worthy

---

[311] Ibid., 161.
[312] Ibid., 1746.

to be "classified" in the same category as the Mother of God. Whatever the case may be, the closest St. Faustina came to calling herself a lily can be seen in her poetic praise of the virginal soul. In this most beautiful of poems, she noted that the virgin is a snow-white lily, as Mary is *the* Snow-White Lily:

> O virgin, lovely flower,
> You will not remain much longer in this world.
> Oh, how beautiful your loveliness,
> My pure bride!
>
> No numbers can count you.
> How dear is your virginal flower!
> Your brightness is in no way dimmed;
> It is brave, strong, invincible.
>
> The very blaze of the noon-day sun
> Dims, and darkens in the presence of a virgin's heart.
> I see nothing greater than virginity.
> It is a flower taken from the Divine Heart.
>
> O gentle virgin, fragrant rose,
> Although there are many crosses on earth,
> No eye has seen, nor has it entered into the mind of
>   man
> What awaits a virgin in heaven.
>
> O virgin, snow-white lily,
> You live wholly for Jesus alone
> And in the pure chalice of your heart
> Is a pleasing dwelling place for God Himself.
>
> O virgin, no one will sing your hymn.
> In your song lies hidden the love of God.
> Even the Angels do not comprehend
> What the virgins sing to God.
>
> O virgin, your flower of paradise
> Eclipses all the splendors of this world.

And although the world cannot comprehend you,
It bows humbly before you.

Although the virgin's path is strewn with
thorns, And her life bristles with many a cross,
Who is as brave as she?
Nothing will break her; she is invincible.

O virgin, earthly angel,
Your greatness is renowned throughout the Church.
You stand guard before the tabernacle
And, like a Seraph, become all love.[313]

CRYSTAL

All throughout her *Diary*, St. Faustina presents the notion
that God's rays (mercies and grace) come to us through the
Hearts of Jesus and Mary like light piercing a crystal. What this
means is that just as in The Divine Mercy image where the rays
burst out of the heart of Christ "as through a crystal"[314] and
penetrate the viewer, so also Mary's heart acts as a reflector of
the mercies and graces of God, and this is the kind of heart St.
Faustina herself wanted.

Perhaps the earliest reference to the crystal metaphor is
evidenced when Fr. Andrasz, her confessor whom she loved
and obeyed completely, told her in 1933 to "make your life as
clear as crystal before the Lord."[315] This injunction by her
confessor she took seriously, as is evidenced in the many
passages that follow chronologically where she incorporated
this metaphor into her spirituality and devotion. On many
occasions when Jesus told her to be a reflection of His mercy,
He often used the metaphor of the crystal:

Every soul, especially the soul of every religious,
should reflect My mercy.[316]

---

[313] Ibid., 1735.
[314] Ibid., 1553.
[315] Ibid., 55.
[316] Ibid., 1148.

> Chosen souls are, in My hand, lights which I cast into the darkness of the world and with which I illumine it. As stars illuminate the night, so chosen souls illuminate the earth. And the more perfect a soul is, the stronger and the more far-reaching is the light shed by it. It can be hidden and unknown, even to those closest to it, and yet its holiness is reflected in souls even to the most distant extremities of the world.[317]

> Love everyone out of love for Me, even your greatest enemies, so that My mercy may be fully reflected in your heart.[318]

> You are to be My living reflection, through love and mercy.[319]

> My mercy has passed into souls through the divine-human Heart of Jesus as a ray from the sun passes through crystal.[320]

Two symbols intimately associated with her use of the crystal metaphor are the heart and *reflection*. This is perhaps why St. Faustina had such a tremendous devotion to the Heart of Christ and, as we will see, to the Heart of Mary. As a crystal reflects light, allowing it to shine and pour forth streams of light, so St. Faustina understood the Heart of Christ to be the source of light. The following excerpts demonstrate this dimension of her crystal metaphor usage:

> Hail, open Wound of the Most Sacred Heart, from which the rays of mercy issued forth. ...[321]

> I saw the same rays [of mercy] issuing from the monstrance and spreading throughout the church. ...

---

[317] Ibid., 1601.
[318] Ibid., 1695.
[319] Ibid., 1446.
[320] Ibid., 528.
[321] Ibid., 1321.

> Their appearance was bright and transparent like crystal.[322]

> O Jesus, it is through Your most compassionate Heart as through a crystal, that the rays of divine mercy have come to us.[323]

Yet, since St. Faustina's devotion was one of imitation, she also recorded the effect God's rays of mercy had on her heart and how she herself wanted to reflect His mercy in her own heart:

> The presence of God penetrates my heart as a ray from the sun penetrates crystal.[324]

> I want to be completely transformed into Your mercy and to be Your living reflection, O Lord. May the greatest of all divine attributes, that of Your unfathomable mercy, pass through my heart and soul to my neighbor.[325]

> My Jesus, penetrate me through and through so that I might be able to reflect You in my whole life. ... I desire to reflect Your compassionate heart, full of mercy.[326]

> My God, how sweet it is to suffer for You, suffer in the most secret recesses of the heart, to burn like a sacrifice noticed by no one, pure as crystal.[327]

> I expose my heart to the action of Your grace like a crystal exposed to the rays of the sun. May Your image be reflected in it, O my God, to the extent

---

[322] Ibid., 370.
[323] Ibid., 1553.
[324] Ibid., 1814.
[325] Ibid., 163.
[326] Ibid., 1242.
[327] Ibid., 351.

that it is possible to be reflected in the heart of a creature. Let Your divinity radiate through me, O You who dwell in my soul.[328]

These various insights into how St. Faustina desired to be both imbued with the rays of mercy and become a vessel of mercy to others as, for example she understands all holy souls[329] and angels[330] to do, is intimately bound up with how she used the metaphor of the crystal to express both her devotion to Mary and her desire to become like Mary, that is, a pure crystal reflecting the light of God.

Were there no mention of the Virgin Mary in regard to her presentation of the crystal metaphor, there would be an inconsistency in St. Faustina's spirituality. This is due to the fact that whatever St. Faustina noted about God, she always brought in the Marian element, noting how Mary is the one to whom all creatures look in order to become perfect, because she alone is the model of creaturely perfection.[331]

In the numerous sections where she presents Mary as being like a crystal reflecting the rays of God, especially Mary as Immaculate Virgin, St. Faustina understood Mary to act as Mediatrix of the mercies of God.[332] The light of God could penetrate us directly, of course. However, St. Faustina's various insights highlight the profound truth that God desires to give us *all* His graces and mercies through the person (heart) of Mary. The following examples exemplify this understanding of her Marian devotion:

O Mary, Immaculate Virgin,
Pure crystal for my heart,

---

[328] Ibid., 1336.

[329] See *Diary*, 1242, 1488.

[330] See *Diary*, 1676.

[331] Similarly, Pope John Paul II, in a homily given on December 8, 1985, to the Extraordinary Synod of Bishops, noted that it is through the "prism of the Immaculate Conception" that the Church comes to understand itself more fully. See *Extraordinary Synod – 1985: Message to the People of God*. (Boston: Daughters of St. Paul, 1986), 97.

[332] See, my article "O Mary, pure crystal for my heart," *Marian Helper* (Fall, 2004): 17-19.

You are my strength, O sturdy anchor![333]

From today onwards [The Feast of The Immaculate Conception], I am going to strive for the greatest purity of soul, that the rays of God's grace may be reflected in all their brilliance. I long to be a crystal in order to find favor in His eyes.[334]

O radiant Virgin, pure as crystal, all immersed in God, I offer You my spiritual life. ...[335]

O sweet Mother of God ,
I model my life on You. ...
O Mother, Immaculate Virgin,
In You the divine ray is reflected. ...[336]

Through Her, as through a pure crystal,
Your mercy was passed on to us.
Through Her, man became pleasing to God;
Through Her, streams of grace flowed down upon us.[337]

SHIELD

The metaphor of referring to Mary as a shield in the spiritual life is one that is dear to Polish Catholic culture. It is commonly known that during military battles, the Polish knights would carry shields with the image of Our Lady of Czestochowa into battle. Also, during the battle of Vienna, Austria, in 1683, King John Sobieski III wore a shield-like plate of the Black Madonna over his armor.

St. Faustina's use of the shield metaphor followed along the same rationale that men in battle wore a shield of Jasna Gora, namely, for protection against enemies. There can be no

---

[333] *Diary,* 161.
[334] Ibid., 805.
[335] Ibid., 844.
[336] Ibid., 1232.
[337] Ibid., 1746.

doubt that St. Faustina understood herself to be in a spiritual battle with the forces of evil. This is easily seen in the following passage:

> O how sweet it is to toil for God and souls! I want no respite in this battle, but I shall fight to the last breath for the glory of my King and Lord. I shall not lay the sword aside until He calls me before His throne; I fear no blows, because God is my shield.[338]

While asserting that God is her shield, St. Faustina also understood that God gives his protection through the Virgin Mary, and this is why she invokes the special protection of Mary on five separate occasions.[339] Concomitantly, St. Faustina, in order to be protected on the spiritual battlefield often invoked the protection of Mary by employing the shield metaphor:

> You are my strength, O sturdy anchor! You are the weak heart's shield and protection.[340]

> Midst storms, 'tis You [Mary] who teach me to love the Lord, O my shield and defense from the foe.[341]

In addition to these examples, St. Faustina also employed the shield metaphor when seeking to give an understanding of how Mary's maternity is a shield against God's wrath and punishment, not because God is not all merciful, but because God Himself has willed that Mary act toward humanity in this fashion.[342]

---

[338] *Diary,* 450.
[339] See *Diary,* 161, 449, 798, 874, 1114.
[340] *Diary,* 161.
[341] Ibid., 1232.
[342] See *Diary,* 686.

ROSARY

T he historical and theological era in which St. Faustina grew up was one in which the Rosary was the preeminent Marian devotion. In fact, before her birth, Pope Leo XIII had written no less than 11 Rosary encyclicals between the years 1883-1902. In addition to the fact that during the lifetime of St. Faustina Mary stressed at Fatima in 1917 the need to pray the Rosary, this gives historical evidence that St. Faustina lived during a time when the Rosary enjoyed great popularity. It is no wonder then that as a young girl, St. Faustina had a devotion to Mary through the Rosary. As a matter of fact, the Kowalski family prayed the Rosary together.[343]

There are many places in the *Diary* where St. Faustina mentions the Rosary and her frequent use of it in her devotional life. As a member of the Congregation of Sisters of Our Lady of Mercy, part of her religious habit consisted of a rosary, and this was bestowed during the vesting ceremony.[344] Her love of the Rosary was not just limited to the chapel, however. She also prayed the Rosary while walking[345] and while weeding.[346]

Saint Faustina so treasured the Rosary that on one occasion, she asked her Superior for permission to pray the Rosary with arms outstretched (no easy accomplishment!),[347] and desired to make the Rosary an obligatory prayer in the new community she desired to found.[348] Furthermore, because she knew the power of the Rosary as both a source of grace and protection, she often

---

[343] See *SMFK*, 341.

[344] See *Diary*, footnote 73.

[345] See *Diary*, 515.

[346] See *SMFK*, 405.

[347] See *Diary*, 246.

[348] See *Diary*, 547. St. Faustina noted on many occasions her desire to found a new religious community. Besides the praying of the Rosary, the only other Marian dimension of the desired community that St. Faustina mentioned was

encouraged the troubled girls to pray it,[349] prayed it as a source of grace for the dying,[350] and when spiritually attacked by demons she prayed it as a source of protection.[351] In addition, there are many other references to the Rosary in her *Diary*.[352]

Since the Rosary consists in large part of the recitation of the Hail Mary, it is not surprising that St. Faustina also had an explicit love of this biblical salutation. Interestingly, when she wanted to show her love for the Immaculate Conception, she recited a novena consisting of 1,000 Hail Mary's, and this she did on at least three occasions. Even in a vision in which she saw St. Joseph and is instructed by him in the spiritual life, he encouraged her, among other things, to pray the Hail Mary.[353] Further illustrating the point, she noted that when she was disturbed, the simple recitation of one Hail Mary often gave her peace.[354]

MARY'S IMMACULATE HEART

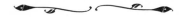

In her love and devotion to the Mother of God, St. Faustina often expressed a special devotion and closeness to the heart of Mary, and on two occasions she even referred to Mary's Immaculate Heart.[355] Devotion to the Immaculate Heart was also a significant devotional dimension in the lives of Christians

---

the following: "The most holy Mother of God will be the superioress of the convent, and we shall be Her faithful daughters." See *Diary*, 568. For various descriptions of this desired community, see *Diary*, 435-438, 536-559, 565, 664.

[349] See *SMFK*, 444.

[350] See *Diary*, 314.

[351] See *Diary*, 412.

[352] See *Diary*, 489, 709, 696, 810.

[353] See *Diary*, 1203.

[354] See *Diary*, 835.

[355] See *Diary*, 805, 1097.

in the early twentieth century, especially due to the revelations at Fatima.

In continuity with her metaphor of the crystal, and how she often portrayed the heart as the place of connection between God and man (graces and mercies given to the sinner), St. Faustina also saw the heart of Mary as a channel of graces:

> I saw, between heaven and earth, the Mother of God, clothed in a bright robe. She was praying with Her hands folded on Her bosom, Her eyes fixed on Heaven. From Her Heart issued forth fiery rays, some of which were turned toward Heaven while others were covering our country.[356]

Mary's heart, in the mind of St. Faustina, serves as a mediation point between heaven and earth, and this because she is Mother of God and our spiritual mother. When she wrote about the heart of Mary in relation to God, she most often placed it within the context of the Incarnation, noting that "the fire of God's love burned in her heart at the Incarnation,"[357] that "her pure heart opens with love for the coming of the Word" because it is "worthy of God Himself"[358] and, finally, that her heart was "Jesus' first tabernacle on earth."[359]

In close connection with her devotion to the heart of Mary is the fact that St. Faustina portrayed Mary's heart as being filled with emotions and passions. For example, she underscores the following emotions in regard to Mary's heart: peace,[360] sorrow,[361] and anxiety.[362] Furthermore, in order to express her filial devotion to the Mother of God, she expressed in tender terms how she took comfort in the heart of Mary:

> I felt the force of Her Immaculate Heart which was

---

[356] *Diary,* 33.

[357] Ibid., 1114.

[358] Ibid., 1746.

[359] Ibid., 161.

[360] See *Diary,* 1097, 1710.

[361] See *Diary,* 786.

[362] See *Diary,* 1437.

communicated to my soul.[363]

I am quite at peace, close to Her Immaculate Heart. Because I am so weak and inexperienced, I nestle like a little child close to Her heart.[364]

When the conversation [with the Mother of God] ended, She pressed me to Her Heart and disappeared.[365]

MARIAN NOVENAS

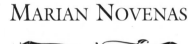

In her many supplications to the Mother of God, St. Faustina often implored her intercession through the devotional practice of novenas. As a devotional formula in which a person enters into a period of prayer lasting for nine days, a novena implies that the need of the petitioner is above the normal request and requires a more extended time of petition.

As a religious community, the Congregation of Sisters of Our Lady of Mercy have in their communal prayer book a plethora of novenas to the Virgin Mary, for example, the novena to the Immaculate Conception and the novena for the Patronal Feast of Our Lady of Mercy.[366] In addition to these required Marian novenas, St. Faustina also made novenas to Mary on her own when there was either a special need or she wanted to express a particular devotion to Mary.

One of the Marian novenas that St. Faustina noted she undertook was a novena to Our Lady of Ostra Brama, which

---

[363] *Diary,* 805.
[364] Ibid., 1097.
[365] Ibid., 1415.
[366] See *TPZ,* 83-84, 110.

was done every year in preparation for the Feast.[367] This novena was one in which many people participated with great fervor. The fact that St. Faustina participated in it with all the other people shows that she not only had an interior devotion to Mary, but also an exterior devotion. On another occasion, when her confessor asked her for prayers, she immediately began a novena to the Mother of God asking for graces for him.[368] Also, she makes mention of a novena she undertook in 1937 in honor of the Assumption of Mary for the three specific intentions of: seeing Fr. Michael Sopocko, for God to hasten the work of mercy, and for Poland.[369]

The greatest expression of her love for praying novenas to Mary is undoubtedly her heroic novenas made in preparation for the Solemnity of the Immaculate Conception. These novenas consisted of the recitation of 1,000 Hail Mary's every day for nine consecutive days, totaling 9,000 Hail Marys! In 1937, she noted that she made this type of novena to Mary on at least three occasions, one of which was when she lie ill in bed.

MARIAN CONSECRATION

The theme of Marian consecration is strong in the devotional spirituality of St. Faustina. Consecration to Mary was a part of the spirituality of the Congregation of Sisters of Our Lady of Mercy, and St. Faustina was a faithful daughter of this devotional practice. In addition, Fr. Andrasz seems to have recommended to her that she give everything to the Virgin

---

[367] See *Diary*, 529.

[368] See *Diary*, 330.

[369] See *Diary*, 1206.

Mary, when in 1937, he told her to "place yourself in the hands of the Most Holy Mother."[370]

There are many different uses of terminology that St. Faustina employed in her giving of herself to the Virgin Mary. While not using the term "consecration" as such, she did use such words and phrases as: *I offer, I entrust, I give,* and *take me.* These phrases imply the same meaning as the word "consecration," because they are meant to express a total giving of oneself into the hands of the Blessed Virgin Mary so that she might offer all to Jesus. The four expressions of total Marian consecration noted above can be seen in the following consecratory "formulas" of St. Faustina:

> O Mary, my Mother and my Lady, I offer You my soul, my body, my life and my death, and all that will follow it. I place everything in Your hands.[371]

> I steeped myself in prayer, entrusting myself to the special protection of the Mother of God.[372]

> O radiant Virgin, pure as crystal, all immersed in God, I offer You my spiritual life; arrange everything that it may be pleasing to Your Son.[373]

> O Mary, my sweet Mother, I give you my soul, my body and my poor heart. Be the guardian of my life, especially at the hour of death, in the final strife.[374]

> I entrusted my perpetual vows to Her [Mary]. I felt that I was her child and that She was my Mother.[375]

> Mary, Immaculate Virgin, take me under Your special protection and guard the purity of my soul, heart and body.[376]

---

[370] *Diary,* 1243.

[371] Ibid., 79.

[372] Ibid., 798.

[373] Ibid., 844.

[374] Ibid., 161.

[375] Ibid., 260.

[376] Ibid., 874.

What these various expressions of Marian consecration reveal is that St. Faustina knew she could totally consecrate herself to the Mother of God — body, soul, and heart — because Mary was also the spiritual mother of St. Faustina, who had been given the capacity by God to receive such an offering.

SORROWS OF MARY

O ver the centuries, there has tended to be an emphasis on the sorrows on Mary in Polish Marian devotion, and often this aspect is applied to the Czestochowa image, even giving her the name of the Sorrowful Queen of Poland. In the life of St. Faustina, she also seems to have had an awareness of, and devotion to, the sorrows of Mary. On three separate occasions, St. Faustina related accounts where she had an insight, saw a vision of the sorrowful Mother, or heard from Mary herself about her tremendous sorrow.

These episodes were reminders to St. Faustina of Mary's great love for humanity and her desire to lead all souls to Jesus. St. Faustina, for her part, sought to bring consolation to the Mother of God through her faithfulness to her divine Son and the mission He had given to her.

The three excerpts where she mentioned the sorrows of Mary are as follows:

> In the evening, I saw the Mother of God, with Her breast bared and pierced with a sword ... I kept praying incessantly for Poland, for my dear Poland, which is so lacking in gratitude for the Mother of God.[377]

---

[377] Ibid., 686.

> Know, my daughter, that although I was raised to
> the dignity of Mother of God, seven swords of pain
> pierced My heart.[378]

> O Mary, today [Presentation in the Temple] a
> terrible sword has pierced Your holy soul. Except
> for God, no one knows of Your suffering.[379]

These three passages share the reference to the 'sword'
piercing the heart and soul of Mary. Obviously, this is a reference to the prophecy of Simeon (Lk. 2:35) and further illus-
trates that St. Faustina's devotion to the Mother of God was
well-grounded in what Divine Revelation tells us about Mary.

---

[378] Ibid., 786.
[379] Ibid., 915.

CONCLUSION

At the heart of St. Faustina's relationship with Mary was the fact that she understood Mary as her most loving spiritual mother who always guided her closer to Jesus and the mystery of trust. As the model and mirror of the spiritual journey, Mary helped St. Faustina to become holy, pure, and immaculate. It is for this reason that St. Faustina entrusted her entire life into the most loving hands of the Virgin Mary.

The Mariological doctrine contained in the Christian spirituality of St. Faustina is both rich and extensive. Though not an academic theologian, she was able to express through her use of prose and poetic-style praise, a deep awareness of the doctrinal truths that saints have honored since the new covenant was established. Of particular note in regard to dogmatic Mariology is the fact that St. Faustina understood Mary to be a constant intercessor with God for the benefit of humanity. Mary fulfills this role because she is the merciful Queen-Mother who never forgets the struggle of her people.

The devotional life of St. Faustina was also of exceptional quality. Her tender and affectionate dialogues with the Mother of God display an intimacy with the Blessed Virgin rarely experienced by those on the path to holiness. Furthermore, her various ways of expressing her devotion, especially through the use of theological metaphors — for example, the lily, the crystal and the shield — exhibit an altogether profound understanding of the filial and devotional life of this great twentieth century saint. It is rare, indeed, that after 20 centuries of Marian devotion, a person is able to contribute such powerful imagery to the area of Marian devotion.

St. Faustina is a model for how a Christian is to entrust himself entirely into the hands of Mary, so as to be a more perfect disciple of Christ. Trust, mercy, love, and surrender to God are only the beginning of the fruits that we, too, shall experience if we seek to imitate the example of St. Faustina and consecrate our entire lives to the Blessed Virgin Mary.

"Jesus, I Trust In You!"

APPENDIX[380]

NOVENA TO THE IMMACULATE CONCEPTION[381]

I greatly rejoice in the Lord
and my soul rejoices in My God.
Because He clothed me with the robes of salvation
and covered me with the cloak of holiness.
Glory to the Father and to the Son
and to the Holy Spirit
as it was in the beginning, now and always,
for all ages. Amen.
You are all beautiful, O Mary.
You are all beautiful, O Mary.
Original sin is not in you.
Original sin is not in you.
You are the glory of Jerusalem.
You are the joy of Israel.
You are the pride of our people.
You are the advocate of sinners.
O Mary, O Mary,
Virgin most prudent
Mother most gracious,
pray for us.
Intercede for us
with Our Lord Jesus Christ.
O Mary conceived without sin
pray for us

---

[380] All of the prayers contained in the Appendix can be found in *TPZ*, and have been generously translated for this book by Fr. Martin Rzeszutek, MIC.

[381] This novena was prayed by St. Faustina's community during the nine days preceding the Solemnity of the Immaculate Conception (December 8th).

who have recourse to you.
Lord, listen to our prayer,
and let our cry come unto you.
At your Conception, O Virgin, you were Immaculate
Pray for us to the Father to whose Son you gave birth.

Let us pray:
God, who through the Immaculate Conception of the
Blessed Virgin Mary prepared a worthy dwelling place for
Your Son, and by the foreseen death of Your Son, preserved
her from every stain of sin, grant us by her intercession to
come to You without sin. We ask this through Christ Our
Lord. (Litany of Loreto to follow.)

ACT OF ELECTION OF THE MERCIFUL MOTHER OF GOD AS THE SUPERIOR GENERAL OF THE CONGREGATION[382]

Mary, Mother of Mercy, we, your Congregation, united in
one common mind with the Sisters living here on earth and
those deceased in heaven kneel at your feet in humble confidence that you listen to everyone who has recourse to you.

Most Holy Mother, we beg you, take once again into your
hands the helm of our Congregation as our Superior General.
We entrust to your goodness the growth of our Congregation
and ask that it be always in accord with the designs of God. We
dedicate to you the individual sanctification of each one of us
and faithfulness to the grace of vocation until death.

Immaculate Mother of Mercy, we entrust to you our
Superiors and together with them ask for the light to see and
strength in all their difficult and responsible duties. We entrust
into your motherly hands all of our endeavors. Grant that they

---

[382] This is the prayer that was used on August 5, 1937, for the election of the Virgin
Mary as the Superior General in Warsaw. It was prayed by all the houses of the
Congregation on August 15, 1937.

always be undertaken for God's greater glory. We entrust to you the material concerns of the Congregation, that they not overwhelm us and distract us from spiritual and apostolic works. Entrust us to St. Joseph, your spouse, that as a good father he watch over our spiritual and material goods. To you we dedicate our young religious and new vocations. We give to you everyone entrusted to us by God's mercy, especially girls and women who need moral renewal. Mother of Mercy, we beg of you that none of them perish.

Mary our Mother, grant that we live holy lives and die a holy death, that each one of us, according to your wishes, shine with humility, purity, love of God and neighbor, kindness and mercy. We firmly believe that Jesus gave us yourself as Superior and that you accepted to govern our Congregation.

Supported by God's grace we pledge to you, Mary, our Mother General, that we faithfully respond to every call of your Son. We desire by our lives to imitate His stance before human spiritual misery. We promise to instill confidence in God's boundless mercy in this world, especially with regard to those who have doubted it. Grant that we be a living sign of God's mercy in the world, serving the sick, the poor, the neglected, and those most in need. We place our confidence in your motherly mercy. In it we hope to find our support in moments of suffering, in difficulties of life, and at the hour of death.

We render homage to you, Mother of Mercy, our Most Holy Mother General. Rule over us, watch over us, and lead us to God. Amen.

PRAYER TO THE IMMACULATE
MOTHER OF MERCY[383]

Immaculate Mother of Mercy, we turn to your protection, beseeching you as our mother, be always with us and mold our hearts according to your image.

We, your daughters, desire that by our life we serve you faithfully in humility and forgetful of ourselves. And, you, O Mother, enflame our hearts with your burning love of your Son and the souls redeemed by His blood. May not one of these hesitate to offer herself in sacrifice for holy Church, the Holy Father, and souls entrusted to us. Mother of Mercy, give to our Congregation many and holy vocations, that we may always spread trust in God's inscrutable mercy on the world and in your Motherly Mercy in which we may find support in life and the hour of death. Amen.

---

[383] In preparation for the Feast of Our Lady of Mercy (August 5), the Sisters made a novena consisting of the above prayer and the "Chaplet to the Merciful Mother of God".

ABOUT THE AUTHOR

Fr. Donald H. Calloway, MIC, a convert to Catholicism, is a member of the Congregation of Marians of the Immaculate Conception. He holds a B.A. from Franciscan University of Steubenville, M.Div. and S.T.B. degrees from the Dominican House of Studies in Washington, D.C., and an S.T.L. in Mariology from the International Marian Research Institute in Dayton, OH. He has written articles for *Homiletic & Pastoral Review* and *Ephemerides Mariologicae,* and is the editor of two books: *The Immaculate Conception in the Life of the Church* (Stockbridge, MA: Marian Press, 2004), and *The Virgin Mary and Theology of the Body* (Stockbridge, MA: Marian Press, 2005). Fr. Calloway is currently the House Superior of the Marian House of Studies in Steubenville, OH.

Books by
Fr. Donald H. Calloway, MIC

The Immaculate Conception in the Life of the Church
(Stockbridge, MA: Marian Press, 2004), 198 pgs

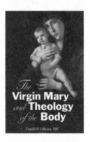

The Virgin Mary and Theology of the Body
(Stockbridge, MA: Marian Press, 2005), 284 pgs

To order, contact:

Marian Helpers Center
Eden Hill
Stockbridge, MA 01263

1-800-462-7426
www.marian.org

PROMOTING DIVINE MERCY SINCE 1941

Marian Press, the publishing apostolate of the Congregation of Marians of the Immaculate Conception has published and distributed millions of religious books, magazines and pamphlets that teach, encourage, and edify Catholics around the world. Our publications promote and support the ministry and spirituality of the Marians of the Immaculate Conception. Loyal to the Holy Father and to the teachings of the Catholic Church they fulfill their special mission by:

- Fostering devotion to Mary, the Immaculate Conception.
- Promoting The Divine Mercy message and devotion.
- Offering assistance to the dying and the deceased, especially the victims of war and disease.
- Promoting Christian knowledge, administering parishes, shrines, and conducting missions.

Based in Stockbridge, MA, Marian Press is known as the publisher of the *Diary of Saint Maria Faustina Kowalska*, and the Marians are the leading authorities on The Divine Mercy message and devotion.

Stockbridge is also the home of the National Shrine of The Divine Mercy, the Association of Marian Helpers, and a destination for thousands of pilgrims each year.

Globally, the Marians' ministries also include missions in developing countries where the spiritual and material needs are enormous.

To learn more about the Marians, their spirituality, publications or ministries, visit www.marian.org, or www.thedivinemercy.org, the Marians' website that is devoted exclusively to Divine Mercy.

Below is a view of the National Shrine of The Divine Mercy and its Residence in Stockbridge, MA. The Shrine, which was built in the 1950s was declared a National Shrine by the National Conference of Catholic Bishops on March 20, 1996.

© MARIE ROMAGNANO

MARIAN PRESS
STOCKBRIDGE
MA 01263
PRO CHRISTO ET ECCLESIA

For our complete line of books, DVDs, videos, and other trustworthy resources on Divine Mercy and Mary, visit thedivinemercy.org or call 1-800-462-7426 to have our latest catalog sent to you.

ESSENTIAL DIVINE MERCY RESOURCES

DIARY OF SAINT MARIA FAUSTINA KOWALSKA: DIVINE MERCY IN MY SOUL, DELUXE LEATHER-BOUND EDITION

Share the gift of mercy with this deluxe edition of the book that has sparked The Divine Mercy movement among Christians. Pages come with gilded edges and a ribbon marker. 7 1/8" x 4 3/8", 772 pages, 37 photos.

BURGUNDY: DDBURG 978-1-59614-189-6
NAVY BLUE: DDBLUE 978-1-59614-190-2

Hardcover, Trade Paper, and Compact Editions available in English and Spanish.

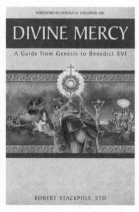

DIVINE MERCY: A GUIDE FROM GENESIS TO BENEDICT XVI

The value of this book by Divine Mercy expert Robert Stackpole, STD, is that the author explores God's mercy throughout salvation history. With this guide, learn what Scripture, the Church's great theologians, the saints, and recent popes have said about the topic. Includes study questions and discussion starters for groups.

AGGB 978-1-59614-185-8